the Carrot Cookbook

By Ann Saling
Drawings by Darci Covington

PACIFIC Search

715 Harrison Street
Seattle, Washington 98109

Cover and Page Design by Lou Rivera

First printing, November 1975
Copyright© 1975 by Pacific Search
International Standard Book Number 0-914718-11-8
Library of Congress Catalog Card Number 75-32835
Printed in the U.S.A.

Table of Contents

Acknowledgments

The author wishes to thank the following friends for recipe suggestions: Hilda Bruer, Ann Cook, Ruth Craig, Mathilde Kendler, Herta Kruger, Ada Kyllonen, Madeleine LHuillier, Helen Newell, Ruth Wiltermood, and Renate York.

An Aphrodisiac Disguised as a Common Garden Root?

The origin of the carrot is wreathed in mystery and controversy. Although carrot remains have been found in Swiss prehistoric lake dwellings, the root is not believed to have been extensively eaten in ancient days. Carrots were planted in the eighth century B.C. Babylonian garden of King Merodach-baladan III. But since they were planted among the scented herbs, it is possible that the root was not eaten at that time.

Some botanists believe that our modern carrot with the large taproot is descended from the wild carrot. Both are members of the Umbelliferae family, a huge family that includes caraway seed, celery, dill, fennel, parsley, parsnip, anise, coriander, and cumin. This family of herbs has been recognized since the time of Theophrastus in the third century B.C.

Pliny the Elder, Roman naturalist and author who died in 79 A.D., wrote: "They cultivate a plant in Syria like the wild carrot, and of the same properties, which is eaten cooked or raw and is of great service as a stomachic (tonic)."

He may have been referring to a parsniplike plant. *De Re Culinaria* (Of Culinary Matters), the earliest existing cookbook (hand-written copies date from the eighth and ninth centuries A.D.), gives the same name for carrots and parsnips.

In ancient Greece, where the carrot was called *Daucon*, it was a popular aphrodisiac, believed to be an effective love potion or philter, inducing in the one who ate it love for a particular person. In sixteenth-century England, the carrot was also considered a love philter: it "provoketh Venus." Even today, the French say that carrots *rendent aimable*: they make you loving.

Seventeenth-century English cooks created elaborate salads, *sallets*, for dining table centerpieces. One recipe describes a castle "carved out of Carrets and Turnips." Another cook whose specialty

5

was sculpting rice, potatoes, and macaroni into culinary masterpieces resembling Wedgwood china, suggested the use of a raw carrot as a whittling instrument in culinary sculpture.

A Frenchman of the famous horticulturist family, the Vilmorin, is often called "the father of the modern carrot." In the 1830s he reportedly changed the stringy root of the wild carrot into the juicy modern carrot by using rich soil. It took three years.

Others give the Dutch credit for improving the carrot, claiming that carrots migrated from Dutch to British gardens during the reign of Elizabeth I. Two decades later, English ladies in the court of Charles I were so delighted with the delicate fernlike foliage of the carrot that they wore it in their hair as decoration.

The carrot made its first appearance in print in thirteenth-century China. After 1536 it was regularly mentioned in European literature. Early American colonists brought carrots with them to Virginia in 1609 and to New England in 1629. Easy to grow and easy to store, the carrot soon became popular with American Indians.

The carrot continues to make occasional news. In World War I the Germans chopped, roasted, and ground up carrots to use as a substitute coffee. Some housewives recycled the "coffee" grounds, using them in place of scarce flour in baking.

In World War II carrots gained fame for supposedly aiding British bomber crews to achieve pinpoint accuracy during night raids over Germany. The British War Ministry encouraged the belief that eating raw carrots to improve night vision before each mission was responsible for the phenomenal results of the bombing raids. But the real reason for their success, which they wanted to keep secret from the Germans, was the newly developed radar.

A revolutionary method of plant propagation, tissue culture, was successfully applied to carrots in 1975. This assures that every plantlet growing from the original cell tissue will be identical. This method involves replanting only the superior roots the second year in order to produce superior seed. Carrots are a biennial, with the thick tap root that has stored up sugary food the first year growing tough and woody the second year as the food goes into flower and seed production. Gardeners grow them as annuals, however, interrupting them in midcycle to harvest the root.

Growing & Cooking Hints

The carrot is the Cinderella of the vegetable garden. This ho-hum, humdrum, "good for you" vegetable is just waiting to be discovered by the imaginative cook whose magic touch will elevate it to regal status. This recipe book tries to transform an unappreciated vegetable into a gourmet's delight.

Available all year long in the food market, carrots are inexpensive, have almost no waste, and are easy to grow at home and to store. They are an excellent source of carotene (provitamin A). Low in calories, they are a dieter's friend. In addition, they add color, texture, and a sweet unobtrusive flavor to a variety of dishes such as candies, cakes, pickles, and beverages. Carrot tops are not used as food because they can cause stomach upset. However, the very young tops can be dried for use as a tea. The mature tops yield a bright greenish yellow dye for home spinners.

Carrots require little space in the garden. They can even be grown in a narrow strip along the flower beds where their delicate foliage adds a decorative touch. Sunshine and a light soil are their principal requirements. If your soil is heavy, choose the short blunt varieties like Danvers Half Long and Nantes. Cultivate the soil deeply, removing stones and breaking up clods.

Sowed successively, carrots will yield from about mid-June to November. For patio gardeners, there are miniature varieties, full grown at three or four inches; for instant gardeners, there are carrot seed tapes; for children, who are impatient gardeners, there are the tiny "fingerlings", which make delicious eating. The foliage can be used in flower arrangements.

Carrots are not really hardy, so pull them before an anticipated heavy frost, first loosening the ground with a pitch fork. Before storing, leave them in the sun for a few hours to destroy soil bacteria that might later cause rot. Remove the leafy tops to conserve vitality. They will keep three to four months in a root cellar or ground pit, in slightly dampened sand or straw, or in the refrigerator crisper in a plastic bag with a few ventilation holes. In regions with mild winters, the easiest way to store carrots is to leave them in the ground. Cut the tops off and cover the carrots with a heavy mulch. They will keep all winter.

Most of these recipes call for raw carrots because of the ease of preparation and the texture they add to recipes. Generally, however, raw or cooked carrots can be interchanged. Vary the cutting: slice them diagonally, in rounds, lengthwise, or use a French cutter for a corrugated look. Young whole carrots are a special delicacy; large ones cooked whole in a pressure cooker require only about five minutes.

Raw carrots yield different textures depending upon how you shred them. For a fine texture, grate them on the third coarsest side of a four-sided grater. For "shredded and chopped", shred the carrots coarsely on the second coarsest side of the four-sided grater, and then quickly chop them with a heavy knife or cleaver. Blender-chopped carrots are a bit chunkier when whirled only a few seconds, always with liquid, and in small amounts. They can also be almost liquified in a blender. For carrot juice an electric juice extractor is ideal.

Spice up your life and your table with the Cinderella vegetable from the carrot patch!

Appetizers
Beverages
Breads

GUACAMOLE

AVOCADOS   2, peeled and mashed
LEMON or LIME JUICE   2 tablespoons
SALT   ½ teaspoon
PEPPER   ½ teaspoon
GREEN ONIONS WITH TOPS   3, chopped
MEDIUM TOMATO   ½, peeled and chopped
CARROTS   ½ cup chopped
MAYONNAISE   2 tablespoons
WORCESTERSHIRE SAUCE   1 teaspoon
TABASCO SAUCE   several drops
COTTAGE CHEESE   1 cup (optional)

Whirl all ingredients together briefly in blender. Serve soon after mixing. Makes 3 cups.

BLUE CHEESE COCKTAIL BALL

BLUE CHEESE   2 tablespoons crumbled
CHIVE or PIMENTO CREAM CHEESE   1 8-ounce package
MARGARINE   3 tablespoons
SALMON   1 7-ounce can, drained and flaked
CARROTS   ⅓ cup finely grated
RIPE OLIVES   ¼ cup chopped
CHIVES   1 tablespoon chopped
WORCESTERSHIRE SAUCE   1 teaspoon
GARLIC SALT   ¼ teaspoon
LEMON JUICE   2 teaspoons
ONION   1 teaspoon grated
WALNUTS   ½ cup chopped
PARSLEY   3 tablespoons chopped

Cream blue cheese, cream cheese, and margarine. Add rest of ingredients except nuts and parsley. Press into a roll or ball, and chill. After chilling, roll in nuts and/or parsley.

SWEET PICKLED CARROT STICKS

VINEGAR   1 cup
WATER   1 cup
SUGAR   3 cups
PICKLING SPICES   2 tablespoons in cheesecloth bag
CARROTS   4 cups cut in sticks and cooked until nearly tender

Boil vinegar, water, sugar, and spices together for 30 minutes. (For stronger syrup, omit water.) Let carrots stand in hot syrup overnight. Then bring to a boil and boil for 5 minutes. Remove spice bag and pack carrots into 3 sterilized pint jars, filling to top with syrup. Seal.

Dill Pickled Carrot Sticks: *Instead of pickling spices, use ½ teaspoon each of celery seed, caraway seed, mustard seed, and dill seed. Do not remove seeds after boiling.*

OREGANO MARINADE

WINE VINEGAR or LEMON JUICE   ¼ cup
VEGETABLE OIL   ¼ cup
SUGAR   ¼ cup
OREGANO   ½ teaspoon
TABASCO SAUCE   several drops
PREPARED MUSTARD   1 teaspoon
GARLIC CLOVE   1, minced
SALT   1 teaspoon
PARSLEY   1 tablespoon chopped
CARROTS   2 cups small whole carrots or julienned cooked until barely tender.

Mix all ingredients together except carrots. Soak carrots in marinade for several hours or overnight. Invert occasionally. Use as appetizers or in salad. Makes 2 cups.

LUNCH MEAT ROLLS

SHARP CHEDDAR CHEESE   ½ cup shredded
CELERY   ¼ cup minced
PREPARED MUSTARD   ½ teaspoon
PICKLE RELISH   3 tablespoons
MAYONNAISE   2 tablespoons
LUNCH MEAT SLICES   6
CARROTS   6 julienne strips, cooked
DILL WEED or PARSLEY   chopped

Mix first 5 ingredients well. Spread mixture on each meat slice; top with a strip of carrot. Roll up and secure with a decorative toothpick. Sprinkle with dill weed. Serve whole or in bite-size slices, each with its toothpick. Makes 6 whole rolls or 2 dozen snack-size.

Note: *Top meat with slice of cheese and carrot. Mix mustard, mayonnaise, and relish; spread on. Roll up as above. Can be baked in foil at 350° for 15 minutes.*

MARINATED TOMATO CARROTS

CONDENSED CREAM OF TOMATO SOUP   1 10½-ounce can
MEDIUM ONION   1, chopped
GREEN PEPPER   ½, minced
SUGAR   ¾ cup
PREPARED MUSTARD   ½ teaspoon
WINE VINEGAR   ⅓ cup
SALT   1 teaspoon
VEGETABLE OIL   ½ cup
WORCESTERSHIRE SAUCE   1 teaspoon
CARROTS   4 cups cooked and sliced or in sticks

Simmer all ingredients together, except carrots, for 5 minutes. Pour sauce over carrots and let marinate in refrigerator overnight. Makes 4 cups.

MARINATED DILL CARROTS

DILL PICKLE JUICE   1 cup
DILL WEED   1 tablespoon
GARLIC SALT   ¼ teaspoon
OLIVE OIL   1 tablespoon
CARROTS   2 cups cooked and cut in julienne strips

Mix all ingredients together and let carrots marinate in refrigerator overnight. Makes 2 cups.

Note: *Use marinated carrots for salads or as cocktail tidbits.*

TUNA SPREAD

TUNA   ½ cup drained and flaked
CARROTS   ⅓ cup cooked and mashed
MAYONNAISE   3 tablespoons
LEMON JUICE   1 tablespoon
STUFFED GREEN OLIVES   2 tablespoons chopped
WORCESTERSHIRE SAUCE   ⅛ teaspoon

Mix all ingredients and chill. Makes 1 cup.

BACON 'N EGG SPREAD

MAYONNAISE   ½ cup
WHOLE EGGS   3, hard-cooked and quartered
BACON SLICES   8, fried and crumbled
TOMATO PASTE   1 6-ounce can
CARROTS   ½ cup shredded
GREEN PEPPER   ¼
SALT   ¼ teaspoon

Mix all ingredients together in blender. Makes 2 cups.

TUNA-HORSERADISH SPREAD

TUNA   1 7-ounce can, drained and flaked
CELERY STALK   1, chopped
CARROTS   ½ cup chopped
MAYONNAISE   3 tablespoons
MARGARINE   ⅓ cup
PREPARED HORSERADISH   1 to 2 tablespoons drained
WORCESTERSHIRE SAUCE   1 teaspoon

Mix all ingredients together in blender. Makes 2 cups.

EGG CURRY

MAYONNAISE   ½ cup
ONION   2 tablespoons chopped
DRY MUSTARD   ¼ teaspoon
SALT   1 to 2 teaspoons
CELERY   ½ cup chopped
CARROTS   ½ cup chopped
PARSLEY   1 tablespoon
TABASCO SAUCE   ⅛ teaspoon
CURRY POWDER   ½ teaspoon
WHOLE EGGS   3, hard-cooked and finely chopped

Mix all ingredients in blender except eggs. Then fold in eggs. Chill well. Makes 2 cups.

BIRDS' NESTS

Very fine, long strips of carrots, either raw or sauteed in butter or a little chicken or beef broth, can make attractive, nutritious nests for creamed foods. Fill them with cream cheese, eggs dipped in chopped parsley, a deviled egg, creamed seafood, or minted peas.

CLAM DIP

COTTAGE CHEESE   1 cup
YOGURT   1 cup
CARROTS   ½ cup shredded and chopped
MAYONNAISE   ¼ cup
GREEN ONIONS WITH TOPS   2, chopped
PARSLEY   1 tablespoon finely chopped
WHOLE EGG   1, hard-cooked and finely chopped
CLAMS   ½ cup drained and chopped

Mix by hand or in blender. Makes 2½ cups.

VEGETABLE DIP

COTTAGE CHEESE   1 cup
MAYONNAISE or HALF-AND-HALF   ¼ cup
CARROTS   ½ cup blender-chopped
ONION   ¼ cup grated
PARSLEY   1 tablespoon finely chopped
RADISHES   2, sliced
CARAWAY SEED   1 tablespoon (optional)
SALT   ½ teaspoon
CHIVES   1 tablespoon

*Mix all ingredients well and chill. Whirl in blender if desired. Makes
2 cups.*

Note: *Vary it by varying the herbs. Dill weed is excellent.*

LO-CAL DIP

LOW-CALORIE COTTAGE CHEESE   1½ cups
YOGURT   ½ cup
LEMON JUICE   1 tablespoon
SOY SAUCE   ¼ teaspoon
ONION   1 tablespoon grated
LEMON RIND   ¼ teaspoon grated
CAYENNE   dash
CARROTS   ¼ cup

Whirl all ingredients together in blender. Makes 2 cups.

DEHYDRATED CARROTS

Carrot shreds can be dehydrated in about 1 hour in a dehydrator or in a warm oven. Place shreds on cheese cloth over a cooky rack and leave oven door barely ajar to let moisture escape. Carrot slices take a bit longer to dry. Dried carrots can be stored in the cupboard in a covered glass jar.

BACKPACK "LEATHER"

CARROTS   2, blender-chopped
APPLE SAUCE   1 pint
WALNUTS   ¼ cup chopped

Mix carrots and apple sauce together. Lightly press walnuts into surface and dehydrate for about 5 hours. Begin processing on plastic wrap over foil. When dry enough, peel "leather" off and dry it directly on screening. Snip into strips with scissors and store in jars.

BLENDER BEVERAGES

Always chop or shred carrots first. Then whirl a small amount of them in blender with a little liquid. Add other ingredients and blend.

EGGNOG

CARROTS   ½ cup chopped
WHOLE EGGS   2
ORANGE JUICE   2 cups
DRY MILK   1 cup
HONEY   2 tablespoons
ICE   ¼ cup crushed

PINEAPPLE-CARROT JUICE

CARROTS   1 cup chopped
PINEAPPLE JUICE   1½ cups
LEMON JUICE   2 tablespoons
HONEY   1 tablespoon

APPLE-CARROT COCKTAIL

CARROTS   1 cup chopped
APPLE JUICE   2 cups
LEMON JUICE   1 tablespoon

TRIPLE GOLD TWIRL

MEDIUM CARROTS   3, chopped
APRICOTS   3
ORANGE JUICE   1 cup

CUCUMBER-CARROT COCKTAIL

CARROTS   2, chopped
CUCUMBER   1, diced
TOMATO JUICE   2 cups
GREEN PEPPER   1, chopped
LEMON JUICE   2 tablespoons
WORCESTERSHIRE SAUCE   1 tablespoon
CELERY STALK   1, sliced
BASIL   generous pinch

Recipes serve 2.

WHOLE-WHEAT BISCUIT BREAD

WHOLE-WHEAT FLOUR   2 cups
FLOUR   ½ cup sifted
BAKING SODA   2 teaspoons
BAKING POWDER   1 teaspoon
SALT   1 teaspoon
LEMON RIND   1 teaspoon grated
YOGURT   1 cup
CARROTS   1 cup blender-chopped
HONEY   ½ cup
WALNUT   ¾ cup chopped
WHOLE EGGS   2

Sift dry ingredients together. Add lemon rind. Mix remaining ingredients together. Add to flour mixture and stir only to blend. Spread batter with rubber spatula in greased 8-inch square pan. Bake at 350° for 25 to 30 minutes. Cut in squares. Keeps very well. Can also be baked as drop biscuits; makes 2 dozen.

YOGURT BREAKFAST BREAD

FLOUR   1½ cups sifted
BAKING POWDER   1 tablespoon
BAKING SODA   1 teaspoon
SALT   1 teaspoon
CINNAMON   ½ teaspoon
NUTMEG   ½ teaspoon
BROWN SUGAR   ½ cup firmly packed
WHEAT GERM   ½ cup
CARROTS   1 cup shredded and chopped
YOGURT   ⅔ cup
VEGETABLE OIL   ¼ cup
WHOLE EGG   1
ORANGE RIND   1 teaspoon grated
WALNUTS   ¾ cup chopped

Sift dry ingredients together except brown sugar and wheat germ. Add them after sifting. Mix together carrots, yogurt, oil, and egg; blend with dry ingredients. Add orange rind and nuts; mix well. Bake in greased 1½-quart ring mold or spring-form pan at 325° for 45 to 50 minutes.

PINEAPPLE TEA BREAD

WHOLE EGGS   3, beaten
BROWN SUGAR   1 cup firmly packed
SUGAR   1½ cups
VEGETABLE OIL   1 cup
FLOUR   3 cups sifted
BAKING SODA   1 teaspoon
SALT   1 teaspoon
CINNAMON   1½ teapoons
NUTMEG   ¼ teaspoon
VANILLA   2 teaspoons
CARROTS   1½ cups shredded and chopped
WALNUTS or ALMONDS   1 cup chopped
CRUSHED PINEAPPLE   1 cup drained
LEMON RIND   1 teaspoon grated

Beat eggs, sugars, and oil together. Sift dry ingredients together and add to egg mixture. Add rest of ingredients. Bake in 2 greased 9 x 5 x 3-inch loaf pans at 325° for 50 to 60 minutes. Cool on rack. Refrigerate loaves when cool.

SPICY CARROT CORNBREAD

WHOLE EGGS   *2, slightly beaten*
SOUR MILK   *1¼ cups*
MARGARINE   *⅓ cup, melted*
YELLOW CORNMEAL   *1½ cups*
FLOUR   *¾ cup sifted*
SALT   *1½ teaspoons*
BAKING POWDER   *2½ teaspoons*
CHILI POWDER   *2 teaspoons*
BAKING SODA   *1 teaspoon*
PAPRIKA   *1 teaspoon*
CARROTS   *1 cup blender-chopped or shredded*
HONEY   *2 tablespoons*
PARMESAN CHEESE   *⅓ cup grated*
GREEN ONIONS WITH TOPS   *¼ cup chopped*

Beat eggs, milk, and margarine together. Add cornmeal sifted with other dry ingredients. Add carrots, honey, and cheese; mix well. Pour into greased 8-inch square pan; sprinkle with onion. Bake at 400° for 25 minutes. This is excellent as a base for creamed foods and for cornbread stuffing.

Note: *For a lighter bread, separate eggs and fold in stiffly beaten whites at last minute.*

BREAD CRUMB PANCAKES

FLOUR   ½ cup
DRY MILK   3 tablespoons
SALT   1 teaspoon
BAKING SODA   1 teaspoon
YELLOW CORNMEAL
DRY BREAD CRUMBS   1 cup
CARROTS   ½ cup shredded and chopped
WATER   1½ cups
WHOLE EGG   1
MARGARINE   ¼ cup, melted
VINEGAR   1 teaspoon

In a measuring cup, put flour, milk, salt, and soda and then fill with cornmeal to 1-cup mark. In a large bowl mix bread crumbs and carrots. Add water (add extra if necessary — batter will be fairly thick), egg, margarine, and vinegar. Mix well. Fry on hot griddle. Makes 12.

OVERNIGHT CARROT-BEER WAFFLES

FLOUR   3½ cups
SALT   1 teaspoon
VEGETABLE OIL or MARGARINE   ⅔ cup, melted
BEER   3 cups
WHOLE EGGS   3
CARROTS   ¾ cup blender-chopped
LEMON RIND   1 tablespoon grated
LEMON JUICE   1 tablespoon
SUGAR   2 tablespoons
VANILLA   2 teaspoons
NUTMEG   ½ teaspoon

Beat all ingredients together with wire whisk until smooth. Let stand overnight in refrigerator or for at least 2 hours. Beer acts as leavening agent. Pour batter into waffle iron thinly. Makes 4 large waffles.

GOLDEN DOUGHNUTS

WHOLE EGGS   3
BROWN SUGAR   ¼ cup firmly packed
VEGETABLE OIL   2 tablespoons
SOUR MILK   2 tablespoons
SHERRY   2 tablespoons
CARROTS   1 cup cooked and mashed
FLOUR   3 cups sifted
SALT   ½ teaspoon
BAKING POWDER   3 teaspoons
BAKING SODA   ¾ teaspoon
CINNAMON   1 teaspoon
NUTMEG   ½ teaspoon
VANILLA   1 teaspoon
ORANGE RIND   1 teaspoon grated
VEGETABLE OIL   for deep fat frying

Beat eggs, sugar, and oil together. Add milk, sherry, and carrots; mix. Sift dry ingredients together; add to egg mixture, kneading if necessary. Add vanilla and orange rind; mix. Chill for 1 hour. Roll out ½-inch thick on floured pastry cloth, and cut with doughnut cutter. Fry in deep fat (265° to 275°). Makes 2 dozen. Good frosted with orange glaze or frosting.

CHEESY CARROT ENGLISH MUFFINS

DRY YEAST   1 packet
WATER   ¼ cup, lukewarm
CARROTS   ⅓ cup sliced
MILK   1 cup
SUGAR   2 tablespoons
SALT   1¼ teaspoons
MARGARINE   ¼ cup
FLOUR   2 cups sifted
WHOLE-WHEAT FLOUR   1 cup
PARMESAN CHEESE   3 tablespoons grated
MARJORAM   ½ teaspoon
THYME   ¼ teaspoon
ONION   2 teaspoons minced
WHOLE EGG   1, slightly beaten
BUTTER
CORNMEAL

Dissolve yeast in water. Chop carrots in blender with milk; then scald. Stir in sugar, salt, and margarine; cool to lukewarm. Mix flours, cheese, seasonings, and onion together. When milk mixture is lukewarm, stir in 2 cups of flour mixture. Add yeast and egg and beat well. Add enough more flour mixture to make a rather soft dough, adding more white flour if needed. Knead smooth for a few minutes.

Put dough in a buttered bowl and butter top lightly. Cover with towel and let rise until double in bulk. Punch dough down, let it rest for 10 minutes, and then roll out ¼-inch thick on pastry cloth sprinkled with cornmeal. Cut in squares or large rounds. Sprinkle with cornmeal, cover with towel, and allow to rise until doubled, about 45 minutes. Fry them on a hot, ungreased griddle, reducing heat after browned, for about 5 minutes on each side. Cool on rack.

Note: These make excellent hamburger buns.

OATMEAL HEALTH MUFFINS

SOUR MILK   1 cup
QUICK-COOKING OATS   1 cup
FLOUR   1 cup
SUGAR   ¼ cup
SALT   1 teaspoon
BAKING POWDER   3 teaspoons
BAKING SODA   ½ teaspoon
ORANGE RIND   1 teaspoon grated
WHOLE EGG   1, slightly beaten
MARGARINE   ¼ cup, melted
CARROTS   ½ cup shredded and chopped
BROWN SUGAR   ¼ cup firmly packed
FRUIT JAM   ⅓ cup (optional)

Pour sour milk over oats and let stand a few hours or overnight. Sift dry ingredients together. Mix remaining ingredients together; blend with oats mixture. Add dry ingredients and mix only until moistened. Spoon into greased muffin pans and bake at 400° for 25 to 30 minutes. Makes 12 medium-size muffins.

GOLDEN NUGGET DROP BISCUITS

FLOUR   1 cup sifted
SALT   ½ teaspoon
BAKING SODA   ¼ teaspoon
BAKING POWDER   ½ teaspoon
MARGARINE   2 tablespoons
CARROTS   ¼ cup shredded and chopped
YOGURT   ½ cup

Sift dry ingredients together. Cut in margarine; then add carrots. Add yogurt, mixing just to moisten. No kneading is required. Drop from spoon onto greased baking sheet or on top of individual casseroles as a crust. Bake at 450° for 10 to 12 minutes. Makes 12.

DINNER ROLLS

WATER   1½ cups, lukewarm
DRY YEAST   2 packets
SUGAR   ½ cup
SALT   1 teaspoon
WHOLE EGGS   2
MARGARINE   ½ cup
CARROTS   1 cup cooked and mashed
FLOUR   6 to 7 cups

Rinse large mixing bowl in hot water. Then pour in lukewarm water and soften yeast in water. Add sugar and salt, stirring with wooden spoon until dissolved. Add eggs, margarine, lukewarm carrots, and 3 cups of flour. Beat with wooden spoon for 3 minutes. Gradually add rest of flour, using enough so that dough is not too sticky. Knead for 10 minutes on a floured board. Let rise until double in bulk. Shape into dinner rolls — crescents, 3-lobed, or oblong — and place on a greased baking sheet (or fill greased muffin pans ½ full). Again, let rise until double in bulk. Bake at 350° for 15 to 20 minutes. Makes 4 to 5 dozen very light rolls.

WHOLE-WHEAT CARROT NOODLES

WHOLE EGGS   3

WATER   3 tablespoons

VEGETABLE OIL   3 tablespoons

WHOLE-WHEAT FLOUR   2 cups

FLOUR   1 cup sifted

SALT   1½ teaspoons

CARROTS   ¼ cup finely grated

PLASTIC WRAP

CORNSTARCH

Beat eggs, water, and oil together with rotary beater until foamy. Mix flours with salt; blend into egg mixture. Add carrots and mix well. Knead on floured pastry cloth for 5 to 10 minutes until smooth, adding more white flour if too sticky. Divide into thirds.

Roll each third as thin as paper between 2 pieces of plastic wrap dusted with cornstarch to prevent sticking. (Do not roll on pastry cloth.) Dough should be very thin and pliable. Remove plastic wrap and hang dough over a straight chair back on a clean tea towel. Turn once when dough begins to dry, in about 1 to 2 hours, depending on the humidity of day. After turning, let it become fairly dry but still pliable, like chamois cloth, and then roll up loosely.

Cut in narrow strips with a very sharp knife. Shake out strips. Boil fresh noodles in chicken broth for 12 to 15 minutes. Or let dry and store in covered jar. These take a bit longer to cook. Makes about 12 ounces (before cooking).

JOGGER'S SNACK CRACKERS

OATMEAL   1½ cups
FLOUR   1 cup sifted
SALT   1 teaspoon
CHILI POWDER   1 teaspoon
CARROTS   3 tablespoons finely grated
ONION   1 teaspoon minced
VEGETABLE OIL   ⅓ cup
WATER   ½ cup
ONION SALT
SESAME SEED
POPPY SEED
PARMESAN CHEESE   grated

Mix first 8 ingredients together, adding more oatmeal if dough is sticky. Form into 2 balls and roll each out very thin on floured pastry cloth. Prick all over with fork. Sprinkle lightly with onion salt. Then sprinkle ⅓ of each rolled out ball with poppy seed, ⅓ with sesame seed, and ⅓ with cheese. Press in lightly. Cut with fancy cutters or make squares by drawing sharp knife down and across. Bake on ungreased baking sheet at 325° for 12 to 15 minutes until lightly browned. Makes 5 to 6 dozen.

DILLED RYE CRACKERS

FLOUR   1 cup sifted
RYE FLOUR   1 cup
VEGETABLE OIL   ½ cup
CARAWAY SEED   1 tablespoon
SALT   1 teaspoon
TARRAGON WINE VINEGAR   3 tablespoons
CARROTS   3 tablespoons finely grated
ONION   1 teaspoon grated
DILL WEED   ½ teaspoon
ONION SALT

Mix all ingredients together except onion salt in a bowl with a fork as for pie dough until dough forms a ball. Add just enough vinegar so that dough holds together. Divide dough in half. Roll each half out very thin on floured cloth. Prick all over with fork. Sprinkle lightly with onion salt. Cut in squares or with fancy cutters. Bake on ungreased baking sheet at 325° for 12 minutes. Do not allow to brown. Cool on rack. Makes 5 or 6 dozen.

CHEESE CRACKERS

FLOUR   1 cup sifted
SALT   1 teaspoon
PAPRIKA   ½ teaspoon
BAKING POWDER   ½ teaspoon
MARGARINE   ¼ cup
PARMESAN CHEESE   3 tablespoons grated
CARROTS   ¼ cup finely grated
ONION   1 tablespoon grated

Sift dry ingredients together. Cut in margarine with pastry cutter. Add cheese, carrots, and onion; blend well. Roll out wafer-thin on floured board, or press out with hands. Cut with diamond-shaped cooky cutter and place close together on ungreased baking sheet. Then cut in half once more to form triangles. Separate them slightly. Bake at 300° for about 15 minutes. Don't let them brown. Makes about 5 dozen.

DUMPLINGS FOR STEW

CAKE FLOUR   1 cup sifted
BAKING POWDER   1½ teaspoons
SALT   ½ teaspoon
CARROTS   3 tablespoons finely grated
MILK   ⅓ cup
VEGETABLE OIL   2 teaspoons

Sift dry ingredients together. Mix carrots, milk, and oil; blend carrot mixture into dry ingredients. Dough will be soft. Drop the dough, a spoonful at a time, onto boiling stew or fricassee chicken in pressure cooker. Put top of cooker on but leave vent off for steaming. Simmer for 15 minutes. Serves 4 to 6.

Note: Whirl carrot mixture in blender if you prefer heavier, richer dumplings. Finely grated carrots make a very light dumpling.

Cakes
Cookies
Candies
Desserts
Pies

VERY AIRY CARROT TORTE

EGG YOLKS   4
SUGAR   1 cup
CARROTS   ⅔ cup very finely blender-chopped
LEMON JUICE   2 tablespoons
LEMON RIND   1 teaspoon grated
MADEIRA or SHERRY   1 tablespoon
VANILLA   1 teaspoon
FLOUR   ½ cup
BAKING POWDER   1 teaspoon
BAKING SODA   1 teaspoon
CINNAMON   1 teaspoon
NUTMEG   ¼ teaspoon
SALT   ¼ teaspoon
EGG WHITES   4
WHIPPING CREAM   whipped
ALMONDS   ⅓ cup slivered and toasted

Beat egg yolks until thick and lemon-colored. Beat in ¾ cup of the sugar, a little at a time, with rotary beater. Add carrots, lemon juice and rind, Madeira, and vanilla; mix well. Sift dry ingredients and add to carrot mixture. Beat egg whites until foamy; add ¼ cup sugar and beat until stiff. Gently fold into carrot mixture. Bake in 2 ungreased, wax paper-lined 8-inch layer cake pans at 350° for 25 to 30 minutes. Cool in pans. To serve, spread whipped cream between layers and on top, and sprinkle with almonds.

RICH CARROT CAKE

FLOUR   2 cups sifted
SUGAR   2 cups
BAKING SODA   2 teaspoons
SALT   1 teaspoon
CINNAMON   2 teaspoons
GINGER   1 teaspoon
WHOLE EGGS   4, beaten frothy
VEGETABLE OIL   1 cup
CARROTS   4 cups shredded and chopped
WALNUTS   1 cup chopped
VANILLA   2 teaspoons

Sift dry ingredients together. Beat eggs and oil together. Gradually beat in dry ingredients. Add carrots, nuts, and vanilla, blending well. Bake in 3 greased and floured 8-inch layer cake pans at 350° for 30 minutes. Cool in pans for 20 minutes. Frost with a cream cheese-butter frosting.

YOGURT-COTTAGE CHEESE CAKE

EGG YOLKS   2
SALT   ¼ teaspoon
LEMON JUICE   2 tablespoons
LEMON RIND   1 teaspoon grated
VANILLA   ½ teaspoon
HONEY   ½ cup
FLOUR   ⅓ cup
NUTMEG   ¼ teaspoon
CINNAMON   ½ teaspoon
CARROTS   ½ cup shredded and chopped
COTTAGE CHEESE   1 cup
BLUEBERRY YOGURT*   ½ cup
GRAHAM CRACKER CRUST   for 9-inch pie (reserve ¼ cup),
unbaked

Beat egg yolks until light and frothy. Blend in salt, lemon juice and rind, vanilla, honey, flour, spices, and carrots. Beat well. Add cottage cheese gradually, alternating with yogurt. Spoon into crumb crust. Sprinkle with remaining crumbs. Bake at 325° for 50 to 60 minutes. Chill.

*Or use other fruit yogurt.

RICK AND MARILYN'S
DATE MAYONNAISE CAKE

BAKING SODA   *1½ teaspoons*
WATER   *1½ cups, boiling*
DATES   *1¼ cups chopped*
WALNUTS   *1½ cups chopped*
FLOUR   *3¼ cups*
SUGAR   *1½ cups*
SALT   *1 teaspoon*
COCOA   *⅓ cup*
CINNAMON   *1½ teaspoons*
MAYONNAISE   *1¼ cups*
VANILLA   *1½ teaspoons*
CARROTS   *1 cup shredded and chopped*

Dissolve soda in boiling water; pour over dates and nuts. Let stand while sifting dry ingredients together. Mix dry ingredients and mayonnaise with pastry blender. Blend in date-nut mixture, vanilla, and carrots. Mixture will be fairly moist. Bake in 2 greased 9-inch layer cake pans at 350° for 30 minutes. A very heavy, rich cake. Frost with a chocolate icing.

TUTTI-FRUTTI CAKE

MIXED CANDIED FRUIT   2 cups chopped
DATES   1 cup chopped
RAISINS   1 cup
SHERRY   ¼ cup
FLOUR   3 cups
BAKING POWDER   2 teaspoons
BAKING SODA   2 teaspoons
CINNAMON   2 teaspoons
SALT   1 teaspoon
VEGETABLE OIL   1½ cups
SUGAR   2 cups
WHOLE EGGS   4
CARROTS   3 cups blender-chopped
WALNUTS   1½ cups coarsely chopped

Soak fruit, dates, and raisins in sherry for several hours. Sift dry ingredients together. In a separate bowl, beat oil and sugar together. Add eggs, one at a time, beating well. Beat until light and fluffy. Gradually add dry ingredients, mixing until smooth after each addition. Add remaining ingredients and mix well. Bake in greased and floured 9 x 13-inch pan at 350° for 45 minutes.

APPLE-APHRODISIA CAKE ROYALE

APPLES   3 cups grated
CARROTS   1 cup grated
SUGAR   2 cups
WHOLE EGGS   2
VEGETABLE OIL   ½ cup
VANILLA   2 teaspoons
FLOUR   2 cups
CINNAMON   1 teaspoon
NUTMEG   ½ teaspoon
GINGER   ½ teaspoon
BAKING SODA   2 teaspoons
SALT   1 teaspoon
WALNUTS   1 cup chopped

Mix apples, carrots, and sugar together. Beat eggs and oil together; add to apple mixture. Add vanilla and mix. Sift dry ingredients together and add to apple mixture. Add nuts; mix well. Bake in 2 greased 9 x 5-inch loaf pans at 350° for 40 minutes.

CHOCOLATE-DIPPED
CARROT-PEANUT BUTTER BALLS

CARROTS ½ cup finely grated
CHUNKY PEANUT BUTTER 1 cup
POWDERED SUGAR 2 cups
MARGARINE ¼ cup
WALNUTS 1 cup chopped
VANILLA 1 teaspoon
CHOCOLATE CHIPS 1 6-ounce package
PARAFFIN 1 tablespoon

Mix all but last 2 ingredients together with hands and roll into balls about an inch in diameter. Chill for several hours. Melt chocolate chips with paraffin (to keep chocolate firmer) in double boiler. Spear each ball with toothpick and dip in chocolate mixture. Chill, pushing each toothpick into egg carton to dry. Keep refrigerated. Makes about 5 dozen.

CHOCOLATE-FROSTED
CARROT-MARSHMALLOW FUDGE

CHUNKY PEANUT BUTTER ½ cup
CARROTS ½ cup blender-chopped
POWDERED SUGAR 1 cup
EVAPORATED MILK ¼ cup
SALT ½ teaspoon
MINIATURE MARSHMALLOWS 1 cup
WALNUTS ¾ cup chopped
CHOCOLATE CHIPS 1 6-ounce package

In double boiler cook peanut butter, carrots, sugar, milk, salt, and marshmallows. Stir until marshmallows melt and mixture is well blended. Mix in nuts. Pour into a buttered 8-inch square pan. Melt chocolate chips in double boiler and pour over top. Chill and cut in squares.

UNCOOKED QUICK NUTTY FUDGE

COCOA   ¼ cup
POWDERED SUGAR   1 pound (about 3½ cups sifted)
CHUNKY PEANUT BUTTER   ¼ cup
VANILLA   1 teaspoon
CREAM or EVAPORATED MILK   2 tablespoons
SALT   ⅛ teaspoon
CARROTS   ½ cup cooked, mashed, and pressed dry between
               paper towels
WALNUTS   1½ cups chopped

Sift cocoa and sugar together. Add peanut butter, vanilla, cream, salt, carrots, and ½ cup nuts. Mix and knead, adding more sugar if necessary. (Less will be required if some of moisture in carrot is pressed out.) Make 2 rolls about 6 to 8 inches long. Roll in remaining chopped nuts. Chill well and slice ½-inch thick. Or press into buttered 8-inch square pan and chill until firm. Cut in squares.

EASY CARROT CANDY

QUICK-COOKING OATS   3½ cups
CARROTS   1 cup shredded, chopped, and pressed dry between
               paper towels
WALNUTS   ¾ cup chopped
PEANUT BUTTER   ½ cup
SUGAR   2 cups
COCOA   2 tablespoons
MILK   ½ cup
MARGARINE   ½ cup

Mix together oats, carrots, nuts, and peanut butter. In a separate pan, boil remaining ingredients together for 1 minute. Combine the 2 mixtures. Press into buttered 9 x 13-inch pan. Chill until firm. Cut in squares.

FRENCH CARROT TRUFFLES

CHOCOLATE CHIPS   1 6-ounce package
MARGARINE   ¼ cup
POWDERED SUGAR   ½ cup
WHOLE EGG   1
VANILLA   1 teaspoon
*CARROTS   ¼ cup cooked, mashed, and pressed dry between
          paper towels*
WALNUTS or PECANS   ¼ cup chopped
MINT or RUM EXTRACT   1 bottlecapful

*Melt chocolate chips in greased double boiler over hot, not boiling,
water. Cream margarine and sugar with pastry blender. Add egg
and beat with rotary beater. (It will curdle.) Then beat in cooled
chocolate and vanilla. Blend in carrots, nuts, and mint. Drop from
spoon onto wax paper and chill for several hours. Makes 2 to 3
dozen.*

RICKY AND ROBBIE'S HONEY CANDY

CHUNKY PEANUT BUTTER   ½ cup
HONEY   ½ cup
WHEAT GERM   ¼ cup
*CARROTS   ½ cup cooked, mashed, and pressed dry between
          paper towels*
POWDERED MILK   1 to 2 cups
WALNUTS   ½ cup chopped (optional)

*Mix all ingredients together except nuts, kneading until smooth. Pat
out in wax paper-lined 8-inch square pan and chill. Cut in squares.
Or form into balls after chilled and roll in chopped nuts (or crushed
granola or graham cracker crumbs).*

MOCK-AROONS

DRY BREAD CRUMBS   1 cup, fine
SUGAR   1 cup
SALT   ¼ teaspoon
CARROTS   ½ cup blender-chopped
WALNUTS   1 cup chopped
VANILLA   1 teaspoon
ALMOND EXTRACT   ¼ teaspoon
WHOLE EGGS   2, slightly beaten

Blend all ingredients together well. Mixture will be crumbly. Using fingers, form mounds on greased baking sheet. Bake at 350° for 12 minutes until light brown. Remove from baking sheet at once to cooling rack. Makes 40 2-inch cookies.

Mock Cinnamon-Aroons: *Add ¼ cup milk and bake in greased 8-inch square pan at 350° for 35 minutes. Sprinkle with powdered sugar and a little cinnamon. Cut in squares and remove from pan at once.*

CARROT-DATE LAYERED BARS

DATES   1½ cups finely chopped
CARROTS   1 cup shredded and chopped
SUGAR   ⅓ cup
HONEY   3 tablespoons
VANILLA   ½ teaspoon
LEMON JUICE   1 tablespoon
ORANGE JUICE   1 cup
ORANGE RIND   1 teaspoon grated
MARGARINE   1 cup
BROWN SUGAR   1 cup firmly packed
SALT   1 teaspoon
FLOUR   1 cup
QUICK-COOKING OATS   2 cups
BAKING SODA   1 teaspoon
WALNUTS   ½ cup coarsely chopped
NUTMEG   ¼ teaspoon

Simmer first 8 ingredients together over medium heat until thickened; cool. Cream margarine and sugar together. Add salt, flour, oats, and baking soda; blend. Press half of this crumb mixture on bottom and up sides of greased 9 x 13-inch pan. Spread cooled carrot-date mixture over top. Cover with walnuts. Press rest of crumb mixture evenly over top and sprinkle with nutmeg. Bake at 350° for 30 to 35 minutes. Cool in pan; cut in bars.

Note: Use a spoonful of date-carrot mixture between 2 3-inch rounds of an unbaked rolled cooky mix. Seal edges, pierce with fork, and bake at 350° for about 15 minutes.

SUN-TANNED PEANUT BUTTER BROWNIES

WHOLE EGGS   2
SUGAR   1 cup
BROWN SUGAR   ½ cup firmly packed
VANILLA   1 teaspoon
CRUNCHY PEANUT BUTTER   ⅓ cup
CARROTS   ½ cup shredded and chopped
FLOUR   1 cup
SALT   ½ teaspoon
BAKING POWDER   2 teaspoons
BAKING SODA   1 teaspoon
CINNAMON   1 teaspoon
QUICK-COOKING OATS   ¾ cup, whirled in blender
CHOCOLATE CHIPS   ½ cup, whirled in blender
WALNUTS   ½ cup chopped

With pastry blender mix together first 6 ingredients until smooth. Sift together flour, salt, baking powder, baking soda, and cinnamon. Blend into egg mixture. Stir in oats, chocolate chips, and walnuts. Bake in greased 9 x 9-inch pan at 350° for 40 minutes. Cut in squares while warm.

DATE-CARROT CHEWS

FLOUR   1 cup sifted
BAKING POWDER   1¼ teaspoons
SALT   ½ teaspoon
WHOLE EGGS   2
BROWN SUGAR   1 cup firmly packed
VANILLA   1 teaspoon
LEMON RIND   1 teaspoon grated
DATES   1 cup chopped
WALNUTS   1 cup coarsely chopped
CARROTS   1 cup blender-chopped
POWDERED SUGAR

Sift dry ingredients together. Beat together eggs, sugar, vanilla, and lemon rind until creamy. Stir dry ingredients into egg mixture. Blend in dates, nuts, and carrots. Bake in greased 8-inch square pan at 325° for 35 to 40 minutes. Cool and cut in bars. Roll in powdered sugar.

GRAHAM CRACKER-CARROT DROPS

CHUNKY PEANUT BUTTER   ½ cup
CONDENSED MILK   1 14-ounce can
SALT   1 teaspoon
VANILLA   2 teaspoons
CARROTS   1 cup shredded and chopped
LEMON RIND   2 teaspoons grated
GRAHAM CRACKER CRUMBS   2 cups
WALNUTS   ½ cup chopped

Blend peanut butter and milk. Stir in rest of ingredients; mix well. Drop from teaspoon 2 inches apart onto greased baking sheet. Bake at 350° for 12 minutes. Makes 4 dozen.

GOLDEN PINEAPPLE BARS

MARGARINE   ½ cup
BROWN SUGAR   ¼ cup firmly packed
FLOUR   1 cup
QUICK-COOKING OATS   ¼ cup
CRUSHED PINEAPPLE or BRANDIED FRUIT   1 cup drained
and chopped

LEMON RIND   1 teaspoon grated
SUGAR   ½ cup
WHOLE EGG   1, well beaten
MARGARINE   1 tablespoon, melted
CARROTS   1½ cups shredded and chopped
WALNUTS   1 cup chopped

Mix margarine and sugar with pastry blender. Add flour and oats;
mix until crumbly. Press mixture on bottom and up sides of greased
8-inch square pan. Prick with fork. Bake at 350° for 15 minutes,
until golden. While crust is still hot, spread it with fruit-lemon rind
mixture. Combine sugar with egg. Fold in margarine, carrot, and
nuts. Spread this over fruit mixture. Bake at 350° for 20 minutes.
Cut in squares.

PINEAPPLE-LEMON SQUARES

SUGAR ¼ *cup*
CORNSTARCH 3 *tablespoons*
SALT ⅛ *teaspoon*
WATER 1 *cup*
LEMON JUICE ⅓ *cup*
LEMON RIND 1 *teaspoon grated*
WHOLE EGGS 2, *slightly beaten*
CARROTS ½ *cup shredded and chopped*
CRUSHED PINEAPPLE 1 *cup drained*
MARGARINE ½ *cup*
BROWN SUGAR 1 *cup firmly packed*
FLOUR 1 *cup sifted*
SALT ½ *teaspoon*
BAKING SODA ½ *teaspoon*
QUICK-COOKING OATS ½ *cup*
WALNUTS ½ *cup chopped*

Combine sugar, cornstarch, and salt. Stir in water mixed with lemon juice and rind. Cook until thick over very low heat or in double boiler for about 7 minutes. Stir a little of the hot mixture into eggs. Add egg mixture to double boiler and cook for 1 minute more. Add carrots and pineapple.

Cream margarine and brown sugar with pastry blender. Then mix in flour sifted with salt and soda until mixture is very crumbly. Add oats and nuts. Pat half of crumb mixture on bottom of greased 9 x 13-inch pan. Spread lemon fruit mixture evenly and sprinkle with rest of crumb mixture. Bake at 350° for 40 minutes until firm. Cool and cut in squares. Serves 10.

GRAHAM-MALLOW CUSTARD

WHOLE EGGS   3
BROWN SUGAR   ¾ cup firmly packed
SALT   ¼ teaspoon
NUTMEG   ¼ teaspoon
ALLSPICE   ⅛ teaspoon
CARROTS   1 cup cooked and mashed
WALNUTS   ½ cup coarsely chopped
EVAPORATED MILK   ½ cup
MILK   ¼ cup
GRAHAM CRACKER CRUMBS   ½ cup
MARSHMALLOWS   10, cut in thirds
WHIPPING CREAM   whipped stiff
NUTMEG

Beat eggs; add sugar, salt, and spices. Fold in carrots and nuts. Scald milk mixture and stir in crumbs and marshmallows. Add slowly to egg mixture. Spoon into 8 greased custard cups. Place in pan of hot water. Bake at 350° for about 30 minutes, until knife inserted comes out clean. Serve with whipped cream sprinkled with nutmeg. Serves 8.

DESERT DELIGHT

WHOLE EGGS   2, well beaten
CONDENSED MILK   1 cup
BAKING POWDER   1 teaspoon
HONEY   2 tablespoons
VANILLA   1 teaspoon
DATES   1 cup chopped
LEMON   1, juice and grated rind
CARROTS   1 cup shredded and chopped
GRAHAM CRACKER or DRY BREAD CRUMBS   ¼ cup fine
PECANS or WALNUTS   ½ cup chopped
WHIPPING CREAM   whipped stiff

In double boiler cook all ingredients together except nuts and whipped cream for 15 to 20 minutes. Add only enough crumbs to thicken slightly. Add nuts. Serve hot or cold with whipped cream. Serves 6.

QUICK PUDDING CRUNCH

BROWN SUGAR   1 cup firmly packed
PECANS or WALNUTS   1 cup chopped
WHOLE EGG   1, beaten
INSTANT BUTTERSCOTCH PUDDING MIX   1 package
LEMON RIND   1 teaspoon grated
MILK   1 cup
YOGURT   1 cup
CARROTS   ½ cup blender-chopped

Mix sugar, nuts, and egg together. Spread mixture on greased baking sheet. Bake at 350° for 18 minutes. Cool and crumble. Divide crumbs in half. Spread half on bottom of buttered 8-inch square pan. Beat pudding mix with lemon rind, milk, and yogurt for 2 minutes until thick. Quickly stir in carrots. Spoon this over crumb mixture in pan. Sprinkle rest of crumbs evenly over top. Chill until firm.

PINEAPPLE FROZEN VELVET

CARROTS   1 cup chopped
HONEY   ½ cup
ORANGE JUICE   ½ cup
LEMON JUICE   3 tablespoons
CRUSHED PINEAPPLE   2½ cups drained
GRAHAM CRACKER CRUMBS   ½ cup
WHIPPING CREAM   1½ cups, whipped stiff
ALMONDS   ¼ cup slivered and toasted

In blender combine carrots, honey, and orange and lemon juice. Whirl until finely chopped. Fold in pineapple and crumbs, and then whipped cream, very gently. Freeze in 2 refrigerator trays. Serve sprinkled with almonds. Serves 8.

SUNNY CITRUS ICE CREAM

CARROTS   2 cups chopped
EVAPORATED MILK   2 cups
LEMON JUICE   3 tablespoons
VANILLA   2 teaspoons
HONEY   ⅓ cup
LEMON RIND   2 teaspoons grated
FROZEN CONCENTRATED ORANGE JUICE   ½ cup

Chop carrots in blender in a small amount of the milk. Add other ingredients and blend until smooth. Pour into 2 small refrigerator trays and freeze. Stir when almost frozen and continue freezing. Serves 8.

DEL'S ORANGE JUICE POPSICLES

CARROTS   ½ cup chopped
CONCENTRATED FROZEN ORANGE JUICE   1 12-ounce can
HONEY   ¼ cup

In blender chop carrots very finely in a little orange juice and honey. Then add rest of juice and honey. Pour into popsicle molds or ice cube trays and freeze. When partially frozen, insert toothpick in each cube. Makes 8 large molds.

ANNIE'S EGGNOG POPSICLES

CARROTS   ½ cup shredded
CONCENTRATED FROZEN ORANGE JUICE   1 6-ounce can
WHOLE EGG   1
VANILLA ICE CREAM   1 pint
MILK   1 cup
NUTMEG   ¼ teaspoon
ORANGE RIND   2 teaspoons grated

In blender chop carrots in orange juice and egg until liquified. Then beat mixture into ice cream with electric mixer. Gradually add milk, nutmeg, and orange rind. Freeze in popsicle molds. When partially frozen, insert toothpick in each mold. Makes 16 large molds.

BRANDIED FRUIT-LEMON PIE

LEMON PUDDING-PIE FILLING   *1 package*
SUGAR   1 cup
WATER   2 cups, cold
EGG YOLKS   2, slightly beaten
MARGARINE   2 tablespoons
BROWN SUGAR   ¼ cup firmly packed
LEMON JUICE   2 tablespoons
LEMON RIND   1 teaspoon grated
BRANDIED FRUIT or CRUSHED PINEAPPLE   ½ cup drained
and chopped

CARROTS   ½ cup shredded and chopped
EGG WHITES   2
PIE SHELL   for 1-crust 9-inch pie, baked
WHIPPING CREAM   whipped stiff
ALMONDS   ½ cup chopped and toasted

Combine pie filling, ¾ cup of the sugar, water, and egg yolks, beating until smooth. Cook over medium heat, stirring until it comes to a boil. Stir in margarine, brown sugar, lemon juice and rind. Cool. When quite thick, add fruit and carrots. Beat egg whites until foamy and then gradually beat in ¼ cup sugar until stiff peaks form. Fold into cooled fruit mixture. Spoon into pie shell. Chill until firm. Top with whipped cream; sprinkle with almonds. Serves 6.

MINCEMEAT PIE DELUXE

SUGAR   ½ cup
HONEY   ½ cup
SALT   ½ teaspoon
MARGARINE   ⅓ cup
WHOLE EGGS   2, beaten
RAISINS   ½ cup
MINCEMEAT   ¾ cup
CARROTS   1 cup blender-chopped
WALNUTS or PECANS   ½ cup
VANILLA   1 teaspoon
LEMON JUICE   1 tablespoon
LEMON RIND   2 teaspoons grated
PASTRY   for 2-crust 9-inch pie

Mix sugar, honey, salt, and margarine in a saucepan and bring to a boil. Combine eggs with remaining ingredients. Add the hot sugar mixture gradually. Cool. Spoon into pastry-lined pie pan. Cover with top crust; seal edges. Cut slits in top. Bake at 425° for 35 minutes. Serves 6.

GRANDMA'S CUSTARD PIE

CARROTS   2 cups cooked and mashed
EVAPORATED MILK   1 cup
ORANGE JUICE   ⅓ cup
WHOLE EGGS   2, slightly beaten
YOGURT or DAIRY SOUR CREAM   ¼ cup
BROWN SUGAR   ⅔ cup firmly packed
HONEY   ⅓ cup
CINNAMON   1 teaspoon
GINGER   ¼ teaspoon
NUTMEG   ¼ teaspoon
ORANGE RIND   1 teaspoon grated
SALT   ¾ teaspoon
BOURBON   1 tablespoon (optional)
VANILLA   1 teaspoon
PECANS or WALNUTS   ½ cup chopped
PASTRY   for 1-crust 9-inch pie with
LEMON RIND   1 teaspoon grated and added to pastry

Mix all ingredients except nuts together in order given, beating well.
Spoon into pastry-lined pie pan. Bake at 400° for 10 minutes.
Sprinkle with nuts. Then lower heat to 325° for another 45 minutes
until firm. Serves 6.

Carrot-Fruit Custard Pie: *Reduce amount of carrots to 1 cup. Add 1
cup crushed pineapple or brandied fruit, well drained and chopped.*

GOLD DUST PECAN PIE

MARGARINE   ¼ cup
BROWN SUGAR   ⅔ cup firmly packed
FLOUR   ¼ cup
SALT   ¼ teaspoon
LIGHT CORN SYRUP   1 cup
VANILLA   1 teaspoon
CARROTS   1 cup shredded and chopped
ORANGE   1, juice and grated rind
WHOLE EGGS   3, well beaten
PECANS   1 cup halved
PASTRY   for 1-crust 9-inch pie

Cream margarine and sugar; add flour. Stir in salt, corn syrup, vanilla, carrots, orange juice and rind. Add eggs and mix well. Sprinkle half of pecans in pastry-lined pie pan. Spoon filling in. Sprinkle with rest of pecans. Bake at 350° for 50 to 60 minutes. Cool well before serving. Serves 6.

CRUSTY ICE CREAM PIE

VANILLA ICE CREAM   1 quart
CARROTS   1½ cups cooked, mashed, and pressed dry between paper towels
BROWN SUGAR   ½ cup firmly packed
SALT   ½ teaspoon
CINNAMON   ½ teaspoon
GINGER   ¼ teaspoon
LEMON RIND   2 teaspoons grated
GRAHAM CRACKER CRUST   for 9-inch pie, baked with
WALNUTS   ½ cup chopped and added to crust

Let ice cream sit at room temperature until begins to soften. Mix with other ingredients and stir. Spoon into cooled pie shell. Freeze until not quite hard. If it becomes hard, let stand 15 to 20 minutes before serving. Serves 6.

Meatless Main Dishes

SCALLOPED CUSTARD

ONION   1½ cups thinly sliced
GREEN PEPPER   ¼, minced
MARGARINE   4 tablespoons
CARROTS   3 cups cooked and sliced
WHOLE EGGS   3, well beaten
SALT   1 teaspoon
DRY MUSTARD   ½ teaspoon
SUGAR   1 teaspoon
DRY BREAD CRUMBS   ½ cup
MARGARINE   3 tablespoons
ROSEMARY   ½ teaspoon
SHARP CHEDDAR CHEESE   1 cup shredded
EVAPORATED MILK or YOGURT   1 cup
MARGARINE

Saute onion and green pepper in margarine. Add carrots to eggs; mix in salt, mustard, and sugar. Blend in onion mixture. Spoon half of carrot mixture into greased 2-quart casserole.

Saute crumbs in margarine; add rosemary. Spread half of crumbs on carrot layer and sprinkle with cheese. Layer rest of carrot mixture. Pour milk over it. Top with remaining crumbs and dot with margarine. Bake at 350° for 25 to 30 minutes. Serves 8.

COTTAGE CARROTBURGERS

COTTAGE CHEESE   1 cup
CARROTS   1 cup shredded and chopped
WHOLE EGG   1, slightly beaten
DRY BREAD CRUMBS   1 cup
ONION   2 tablespoons finely chopped
PARSLEY   1 tablespoon chopped
SALT   1 teaspoon
WORCESTERSHIRE SAUCE   1 tablespoon
WALNUTS   ½ cup chopped
BREAD CRUMBS   1 cup fine
MARGARINE
BUNS

Combine all ingredients except fine bread crumbs and margarine. Form into 6 patties and coat with the crumbs. Fry in margarine until browned. Serve on buns with all the fixings. Serves 6.

NOODLES ORIENTAL

FRESH MUSHROOMS   ½ cup chopped
GREEN ONIONS WITH TOPS   3, chopped
CARROTS   1½ cups coarsely shredded
MARGARINE   ⅓ cup, melted
SESAME SEED   1½ tablespoons
ALMONDS   ½ cup slivered
SALT   1½ teaspoons
SOY SAUCE   2 to 4 tablespoons
NOODLES   1 8-ounce package, cooked and drained
PARMESAN CHEESE   ½ cup grated

Saute mushrooms, onion, and carrots in margarine in a large skillet until soft but not browned. In a 300° oven toast sesame seed and almonds separately for about 10 minutes until light brown. Add sesame seed, salt, soy sauce, and noodles to carrot mixture. Stir until hot. Spoon into greased 9 x 13-inch baking dish and sprinkle with cheese. Bake at 375° for 10 minutes. Sprinkle with almonds. Serves 8.

NUTTY CARROT LOAF

MEDIUM ONION ½, *chopped*
MARGARINE 3 *tablespoons*
CARROTS 2½ *cups shredded (or cooked and mashed)*
CELERY ½ *cup minced*
SHARP CHEDDAR CHEESE 1 *cup shredded*
DRY BREAD or CRACKER CRUMBS 1 *cup (optional)*
WALNUTS ½ *cup*
SALT 1 *teaspoon*
LEMON JUICE 1 *tablespoon*
PAPRIKA ¼ *teaspoon*
WHOLE EGGS 2, *slightly beaten*
EVAPORATED MILK 1½ *cups*

Saute onion in margarine. Add next 8 ingredients and mix well. Mix eggs and milk; add to mixture. Spoon into 2 greased 9 x 5-inch loaf pans. Set in pan of hot water and bake at 350° for 45 minutes until firm. Use as base for seafood sauce. Serves 8.

MOCK MEAT CUTLETS

CARROTS   *2 cups cooked and mashed*
SHARP CHEDDAR CHEESE   *½ cup shredded*
SOFT BREAD CRUMBS   *¾ cup*
ONION   *¼ cup grated*
WHOLE EGGS   *2, slightly beaten*
WALNUTS   *⅓ cup chopped*
SALT   *½ teaspoon*
PEPPER   *⅛ teaspoon*
MARJORAM   *½ teaspoon*
FLOUR
WHOLE EGG   *1*
WATER   *1 tablespoon*
DRY BREAD CRUMBS   *½ cup*
CORNMEAL   *2 tablespoons*
MARGARINE or BACON FAT   *½ cup*

Mix first 9 ingredients together. Shape into patties 1½ inches across; chill until firm. Dip in flour, then in egg beaten with water, and finally in mixture of crumbs and cornmeal. Fry in sizzling hot margarine on each side. Drain on paper towels. These taste like meat. Makes 8 cutlets.

GOLDENROD POTATO PANCAKES

WHOLE EGGS   2
SMALL ONION   ½, chopped
GREEN PEPPER   1 tablespoon chopped
SALT   1 teaspoon
FLOUR or DRY BREAD CRUMBS   3 tablespoons
SAGE   ¼ teaspoon
BAKING POWDER   ½ teaspoon
POTATOES   2 cups cubed
CARROTS   1 cup sliced

Put all ingredients except potatoes and carrots in blender bowl. Add ¼ cup each of potatoes and carrots. Cover and turn on blender, barely chopping vegetables (or use "grate" setting). Add remaining vegetables; turn on blender, barely chopping vegetables. Do not chop too fine. Drop from tablespoon onto greased griddle. Cook until golden brown; turn and brown other side. Cook until done through. Serve with meat dish. Makes 12.

SUPPER CORNBREAD LOAF

ONION   ½ cup chopped
CELERY   ½ cup chopped
MARGARINE   3 tablespoons
WALNUTS or PEANUTS   1 cup chopped
CORNBREAD CRUMBS   1 cup
CARROTS   1½ cups shredded
SHARP CHEDDAR CHEESE   1 cup grated
EVAPORATED MILK   2 cups
WHOLE EGGS   3, beaten
SALT   1 teaspoon
SAGE   ¼ teaspoon
THYME   ⅛ teaspoon
PARSLEY   chopped

Saute onion and celery in margarine until soft. Stir in nuts, crumbs, carrots, and cheese. Mix milk, eggs, and seasonings; pour over carrot mixture. Let stand until liquid is absorbed. Bake in greased 9 x 5-inch loaf pan at 350° for 50 to 60 minutes. Serve with creamed seafood. Sprinkle with parsley. Serves 6.

CARROT-WINE SHIRRED EGGS

CONDENSED CREAM OF CHICKEN SOUP   1 10½-ounce can
YOGURT   1 cup
WORCESTERSHIRE SAUCE   1 teaspoon
PREPARED MUSTARD   1 teaspoon
TABASCO SAUCE   dash
SALT   ½ teaspoon
CARROTS   ½ cup shredded and chopped
GREEN ONIONS WITH TOPS   2, chopped
DRY WHITE WINE   3 tablespoons
MARJORAM or BASIL   ¼ teaspoon
WHOLE EGGS   6
PARMESAN CHEESE   ⅓ cup grated

Mix all ingredients together except eggs and cheese. Bake in 6 greased individual casseroles at 350° for about 10 minutes, until mixture is piping hot. Then break 1 egg into each casserole and sprinkle with cheese. Bake at 350° for 10 minutes, until yolk is set. Do not overbake; it continues baking after removed from oven. Serves 6.

LOW-CHOLESTEROL OMELET OR SCRAMBLED EGGS

Use only egg whites, adding color and richness by finely grating a tablespoon of raw carrot per egg. Add a dash of Tabasco sauce and a little grated onion.

CURRIED CARROT DEVILED EGGS

WHOLE EGGS   4, hard-cooked and halved
CARROTS   2 tablespoons finely grated or chopped
CURRY POWDER   ½ teaspoon
MAYONNAISE   1 tablespoon
DRY MUSTARD   1 teaspoon
MARGARINE   1 tablespoon, soft
POPPY SEED   1 teaspoon

Remove egg yolks and mash well. Stir in all other ingredients except poppy seed, reserving a bit of carrot to sprinkle on top. Fill egg whites; sprinkle with carrots and poppy seed.

AVOCADO-YOGURT OMELET

GREEN ONIONS WITH TOPS   2 tablespoons chopped
GARLIC CLOVE   ½, minced
MARGARINE   2 tablespoons
SMALL TOMATO   1, peeled and chopped
RIPE OLIVES   6, halved
CARROTS   ½ cup shredded and chopped
WHOLE EGGS   6, beaten
YOGURT   ¼ cup
SALT and PEPPER   to taste
VEGETABLE OIL
AVOCADO   1, peeled and diced

Saute onion and garlic in margarine. Add drained tomato, olives, and carrots. Keep mixture warm while you make the omelet. Combine eggs with yogurt and seasonings. Pour into oiled skillet and cook slowly. When omelet is done, add avocado to carrot mixture and warm for a few seconds. Then spread mixture in the center of the omelet and fold over. Serves 4 to 6.

Main Dishes with Meat Poultry Seafood

EGGPLANT-BEEF BAKE

LARGE EGGPLANT   1, *peeled and cubed*
MARGARINE   ⅓ *cup*
GROUND BEEF   2 *pounds*
MEDIUM ONION   1, *chopped*
PARSLEY SPRIGS   4, *chopped*
BLACK OLIVES   ½ *cup chopped*
CELERY WITH LEAVES   ¼ *cup finely chopped*
GARLIC CLOVE   1, *minced*
CARROTS   1½ *cups shredded*
SALT   1 *teaspoon*
TABASCO SAUCE   3 *drops*
WORCESTERSHIRE SAUCE   1½ *teaspoons*
CONDENSED CREAM OF TOMATO SOUP   1 10½-*ounce can*
CRACKER or DRY BREAD CRUMBS   ¾ *cup*
PARMESAN CHEESE   2 *tablespoons grated*
MARGARINE   3 *tablespoons*

Saute eggplant in margarine for about 10 minutes until not quite soft. In separate skillet fry ground beef until meat loses its red color. Drain off fat. Stir beef into eggplant, and then blend in next 9 ingredients. Simmer for a few minutes. Spoon into a greased 9-inch pie pan. Heat tomato soup and pour over meat-eggplant mixture. Sprinkle with crumbs mixed with cheese. Dot with bits of margarine. Bake at 350° until bubbly, about 15 minutes. Serves 8.

GOLD-FILLED MEAT LOAF ROLL

CARROTS   2 cups cooked, mashed, and pressed dry between paper towels
SALT   ½ teaspoon
WHOLE EGG   1, slightly beaten
DRY BREAD CRUMBS   4 tablespoons
GROUND BEEF   ¾ pound
PORK SAUSAGE   ¼ pound
ONION   2 tablespoons finely minced
SOFT BREAD CRUMBS   ½ cup
WHEAT GERM   ¼ cup
SAGE   ½ teaspoon
WHOLE EGGS   2, slightly beaten
SALT   ½ teaspoon
WORCESTERSHIRE SAUCE   ½ teaspoon
CATSUP   4 tablespoons
BACON SLICES   2

Mix carrots, salt, egg, and dry bread crumbs, adding more crumbs if mixture is too moist. On a piece of wax paper, form mixture into a roll 8 inches long, 2 inches thick. Wrap in wax paper and chill for several hours.

Combine remaining ingredients except catsup and bacon. On a piece of wax paper, pat out meat mixture into an 8-inch square, ½-inch thick. Place chilled carrot roll in center and bring edges up around it, pressing together. Lift on wax paper and place roll, seam side down, in greased 9 x 13-inch pan. Discard wax paper. Spread catsup on top and lay bacon strips over it. Bake at 350° for 1 hour. Serves 6 to 8.

BLUE CHEESE-HAMBURGER CASSEROLE

GROUND BEEF   1½ pounds
MARGARINE   2 tablespoons
ONION   ¾ cup chopped
FRESH MUSHROOMS   1 cup chopped
CARROTS   1½ cups shredded
CELERY STALKS   2, chopped
GARLIC SALT   ½ teaspoon
ROSEMARY   ½ teaspoon
PARSLEY   2 tablespoons chopped
CONDENSED CREAM OF CHICKEN SOUP   1 10½-ounce can
YOGURT   1 cup
BLUE CHEESE   1 to 2 tablespoons shredded
CHERRY TOMATOES   1 cup whole
NOODLES   1 8-ounce package, cooked and drained
CROUTONS   1½ cups tiny, cut from stale bread
MARGARINE   4 tablespoons
PARMESAN CHEESE   3 tablespoons grated

In large skillet, fry beef in margarine until almost done. Drain excess fat. Push beef to one side and add onion, mushrooms, carrots, and celery. Fry until softened. Add remaining ingredients except croutons, margarine, and Parmesan cheese. Mix well and heat. Fry croutons in margarine slowly until coated and hot; stir in Parmesan cheese. Spoon meat mixture into large greased casserole; top with croutons. Bake at 350° for about 20 minutes or until piping hot. Serves 8.

SUPER SUPPER SCRAMBLED EGGS OLE

ONION   ¼ cup minced
GREEN PEPPER   2 tablespoons minced
MARGARINE   3 tablespoons
LEFTOVER ROAST, DRIED CHIPPED BEEF, or TUNA   ½
cup cubed, shredded, or flaked
CARROTS   ½ cup blender-chopped
SHARP CHEDDAR CHEESE   ½ cup shredded
MUSHROOMS   1 4-ounce can, drained
PARSLEY   1 tablespoon chopped
TOMATO   1, peeled and coarsely chopped
CHILI POWDER   1 to 2 teaspoons
SALT   ½ teaspoon
PEPPER   ⅛ teaspoon coarsely ground
BASIL   ½ teaspoon
ROSEMARY   ½ teaspoon
WHOLE EGGS   6, well beaten
ENGLISH MUFFINS

Saute onion and green pepper in margarine until soft. Add meat and heat for a few minutes. Add remaining ingredients except eggs and muffins. Heat until bubbling. Pour in beaten eggs and stir carefully until eggs are set. Mixture will be soft. Serve over toasted muffins. Serves 4 to 6.

DEVILED LAMB DELIGHT

MARGARINE   4 tablespoons
FLOUR   4 tablespoons
DRY MUSTARD   1½ teaspoons
LAMB BROTH   2 cups
LEFTOVER LAMB ROAST   2 cups diced
WHOLE EGGS   2, hard-cooked and chopped
CARROTS   ⅔ cup cooked and diced
BLACK OLIVES   ¼ cup minced
WORCESTERSHIRE SAUCE   1½ teaspoons
SALT   ½ teaspoon
GINGER   ¼ teaspoon
MARJORAM   ¼ teaspoon
ONION   2 tablespoons minced
SHERRY or MADEIRA   2 tablespoons
FRESH MUSHROOMS   ½ cup chopped
LEMON RIND   1 teaspoon grated
RICE   cooked
PARSLEY SPRIGS   2, chopped
MINT JELLY

Melt margarine; stir in flour and mustard. Add lamb broth made by
boiling lamb roast bone in water for about 30 minutes. Cook,
stirring, until it thickens. Add all other ingredients except rice,
parsley, and jelly. Simmer until piping hot, stirring occasionally.
Thicken sauce if desired with flour and water. Serve over hot rice
cooked in lamb broth. Garnish with parsley. Serve jelly on the side.
Serves 6.

WHEAT GERM BURGERS

GROUND BEEF   1 pound
CARROTS   1½ cups shredded and chopped
ONION   ½ cup minced
WHEAT GERM   ½ cup
DRY BREAD CRUMBS   ½ cup
SALT   1 teaspoon
PEPPER   ⅛ teaspoon
WORCESTERSHIRE SAUCE   1 tablespoon
PREPARED MUSTARD   2 teaspoons
PARSLEY   2 tablespoons chopped
CATSUP   ¼ cup
WHOLE EGG   1, slightly beaten
VEGETABLE OIL   2 tablespoons

Combine all ingredients except oil. Shape into 10 flat 2-inch patties. Brown on both sides in hot oil.

QUICK MUSHROOM-PORK CASSEROLE

CARROTS   2 cups cooked and sliced
PORK ROAST   2 cups cooked and diced
CRACKER CRUMBS   1 cup, cheesed*
ONION SALT   1 teaspoon
PEPPER   ¼ teaspoon
CONDENSED CREAM OF MUSHROOM SOUP   1 10½-ounce
can
YOGURT   ½ cup
BACON SLICES   2, fried crisp and crumbled

In greased 1½-quart casserole, alternate layers of carrots, pork, and crumbs, sprinkling each layer with onion salt and pepper. Dilute soup with yogurt and pour over casserole. Sprinkle with bacon and bake at 350° for 20 minutes to heat through. Serves 6.

* If you use plain cracker crumbs, add 3 tablespoons grated Parmesan cheese to them.

STUFFED PORK CHOPS

CREAMED CORN ½ cup
DRY BREAD CRUMBS ¼ cup fine
WHOLE EGG 1, well beaten
ONION 2 tablespoons chopped
SAGE ¼ teaspoon
CELERY STALK 1, finely chopped
GARLIC SALT 1 teaspoon
GREEN PEPPER ¼, finely chopped
CARROTS ½ cup shredded and chopped
PARMESAN CHEESE 3 tablespoons grated
DOUBLE-CUT THICK PORK CHOPS 4, cut with pockets
MARGARINE 3 tablespoons

Combine all ingredients except pork chops and margarine and mix well. Stuff chops. Brown them in margarine on both sides, turning carefully. Place in a greased 9 x 13-inch pan; cover with foil. Bake at 350° for 50 to 60 minutes. Serves 4.

CARAWAY PORK CHOPS IN WINE

FLOUR   ¼ cup
SAGE   ½ teaspoon
CARAWAY SEED   3 teaspoons
GARLIC CLOVE   1, minced
SALT   ½ teaspoon
PEPPER   ¼ teaspoon
THICK PORK CHOPS   4
MARGARINE   3 tablespoons
CARROTS   4, halved and cut in fourths lengthwise
DRY WHITE WINE   ½ cup

Mix first six ingredients together. Dip pork chops in mixture and then brown in margarine. Add carrots and barely cover with water. Cook, covered, over low heat for about an hour. Turn chops several times. When water has evaporated, add wine. Bring to a boil and then serve with wine sauce. Serves 4.

Note: Add ½ cup sliced mushrooms to wine sauce.

BEER-BRAISED PORK CHOPS

THICK PORK CHOPS   6
MARGARINE   3 tablespoons
SALT and PEPPER   to taste
BEER   2 cups
ROSEMARY   ½ teaspoon
LARGE ONION   1, thickly sliced
CARROTS   2½ cups sliced lengthwise
BEEF BOUILLION   2 cups
FLOUR   2 tablespoons
WATER   2 tablespoons

Brown pork chops well in margarine; salt and pepper them. Add beer and rosemary, cover and simmer for 30 minutes. Add onion and carrots. Stir in bouillon and cook for another 15 minutes. Blend flour with water and stir in a little of broth from chops. Then stir flour mixture into broth in pan. Cook a few minutes until thickened. Serve meat and vegetables with pan sauce. Serves 6.

HOMEMADE SPICY SAUSAGE

PORK   2 cups cut from uncooked roast
CARROTS   ½ cup chopped
ONION   ¼ cup chopped
GARLIC CLOVE   1 (optional)
PARSLEY SPRIGS   2
SALT   1½ teaspoons
PEPPER   1 teaspoon coarsely ground
PAPRIKA   ½ teaspoon
GINGER   ½ teaspoon
SAGE   ¼ teaspoon (optional)
CAYENNE   ¼ teaspoon (optional)
CHILI POWDER   ¼ teaspoon (optional)

Grind together the pork, carrots, onion, garlic, and parsley. Put through finest blade of grinder twice. Then mix in seasonings with hands. Use all the seasonings for a hot spicy sausage. Chill in refrigerator for 2 days to blend flavors. Shape into cakes and fry.

SAUSAGE SHIRRED EGGS

LINK SAUSAGES   4, quartered
MARGARINE   1 tablespoon
CHICKEN BROTH   ½ cup
WHOLE EGGS   4 (or 8)
SAGE   ¼ teaspoon
SALT   ½ teaspoon
PEPPER   dash
SHARP CHEDDAR CHEESE   ¼ cup shredded
GREEN ONION WITH TOPS   2 tablespoons chopped

Fry sausages in margarine until brown; drain and reserve fat. In each of 4 individual casseroles put 2 tablespoons of chicken broth and 1 teaspoon of sausage fat. Heat in 350° oven for a few minutes until broth is bubbling. Remove and add 4 pieces of sausage to each casserole. Break 1 or 2 eggs into each. Sprinkle with seasonings; then sprinkle with cheese and onion. Return to oven and bake 10 minutes, checking to make sure yolk does not become hard. Serves 4.

CURRIED HAM AND CARROT ROLLS

MARGARINE   3 tablespoons
FLOUR   3 tablespoons
SALT   ½ teaspoon
DRY MUSTARD   ½ teaspoon
CURRY POWDER   2 teaspoons
CAYENNE   dash
MILK   1½ cups
HAM SLICES   6, ⅛-inch thick
PICKLE RELISH   ¼ cup
MEDIUM CARROTS   6, cooked whole
WHOLE-WHEAT BREAD SLICES   6, toasted
PARSLEY SPRIGS   2, chopped

Melt margarine and gradually mix in next 5 ingredients. Gradually add milk, and cook over low heat, stirring constantly, until thickened. Spread ham slices with pickle relish and lay 1 carrot in center of each ham slice. Roll up and fasten with toothpick. Place them side by side in greased shallow baking dish. Pour curry sauce around but not over ham rolls. Bake at 400° for 15 to 20 minutes until piping hot. Serve on toast. Spoon sauce over and sprinkle with parsley. Serves 6.

MEAT LOAF-CHEESE SPECIAL

MEATLOAF   your favorite recipe
SHARP CHEDDAR CHEESE SLICES
DILL PICKLE   ½ cup finely chopped
CARROTS   1 cup cooked and mashed

Place half of meat in a greased 9 x 5-inch loaf pan. Cover with a layer of cheese, dill pickle, carrots, and another layer of cheese. Top with rest of meat. Bake as usual.

RICE-PEANUT LOAF

CARROTS   1 cup blender-chopped
PEANUTS   1 cup blender-chopped
ONION   ¼ cup chopped
RICE   1 cup cooked
GREEN PEPPER   1 tablespoon chopped
EVAPORATED MILK   ¾ cup
WHOLE EGG   1, slightly beaten
PREPARED MUSTARD   ¼ teaspoon
SALT   1 teaspoon
SHARP CHEDDAR CHEESE   ½ cup shredded
MARJORAM   ½ teaspoon
BACON SLICES   3
CARROT-MUSHROOM SAUCE

*Mix all ingredients together in order given except bacon and sauce.
Spoon into greased 9 x 5-inch loaf pan. Top with bacon slices. Bake
at 350° for 50 to 60 minutes. Serve with Carrot-Mushroom Sauce, or
as a base for creamed seafood. Serves 6.*

CARROT-MUSHROOM SAUCE

CONDENSED CREAM OF MUSHROOM SOUP   1 10½-ounce
can

CHICKEN BROTH   1 cup
EVAPORATED MILK   ¼ cup
CARROTS   ½ cup blender-chopped
LEMON JUICE   1 tablespoon
PAPRIKA   ¼ teaspoon
SALT   ½ teaspoon
PARSLEY   2 tablespoons chopped

*Mix all ingredients together and heat just to boiling. Serve over Rice-
Peanut Loaf. Makes 3 cups.*

CHILEAN CHICKEN-STUFFED AVOCADO

HARD-SHELLED AVOCADOS   3
LEMON JUICE   3 tablespoons
CHICKEN   1 cup cooked and finely ground
PREPARED MUSTARD   1 teaspoon
MAYONNAISE   ½ cup
CARROTS   ¼ cup blender-chopped
CHICKEN BROTH   3 tablespoons
BASIL   ¼ teaspoon crumbled
SALT   ¼ teaspoon
ONION   1 tablespoon minced
WHOLE EGG   1, hard-cooked and finely chopped
BACON SLICES   3, fried crisp and crumbled

Halve the avocados and scoop out pulp carefully, leaving a little in shell to firm it. Mash pulp well with lemon juice. Mix chicken with remaining ingredients, reserving a little bacon for top. Blend in avocado pulp. Stuff shells; sprinkle with bacon. Bake at 350° for 10 minutes until piping hot. Very rich. Serves 6.

CHICKEN TIMBALE

CHICKEN BROTH   ½ cup
WHOLE EGGS   3
MUSHROOMS   1 4-ounce can
PARSLEY SPRIG   1, chopped
DAY-OLD BREAD SLICE   1, crumbled
CHICKEN   1 cup cooked and diced
CARROTS   ½ cup shredded and chopped
SALT   1 teaspoon
THYME   ¼ teaspoon

Mix all ingredients together and spoon into 6 greased custard cups. Place cups in pan of hot water. Bake at 325° for about 35 minutes until set. Serves 6.

THANKSGIVING GOLD CASSEROLE

TURKEY or CHICKEN   2 cups cooked and cubed
CARROTS   1 cup shredded
CELERY WITH LEAVES   ½ cup chopped
ONION   2 tablespoons chopped
CONDENSED CREAM OF CHICKEN SOUP   1 10½-ounce can
RICE or NOODLES   2 cups cooked
SHARP CHEDDAR CHEESE   ¼ cup shredded
SALT   1 teaspoon
PEPPER   ¼ teaspoon
LEMON JUICE   1 tablespoon
LEMON RIND   2 teaspoons grated
MAYONNAISE   ½ cup
BACON SLICES   4, fried and crumbled
WHOLE EGGS   4, hard-cooked and diced
WALNUTS   ½ cup chopped
BREAD CRUMBS   buttered and herbed*

Mix all ingredients together and spoon into greased 2-quart casserole. Top with crumbs. Bake at 400° for 20 to 25 minutes. Serves 6 to 8.

*Add ¼ teaspoon thyme or sage to crumbs while sauteing them.

MUSHROOM STUFFED TROUT AU VIN

CARROTS   ¼ cup grated and chopped
GREEN ONIONS WITH TOPS   2, chopped
PIMENTOS   2, chopped
PARSLEY SPRIGS   3, chopped
TARRAGON   1 teaspoon
FRESH MUSHROOMS   ½ cup chopped
TROUT   4 12-inch (or 1 2-pound)
SALT
MARGARINE   3 tablespoons, melted
DRY WHITE WINE   ½ cup
DRY BREAD CRUMBS or CHEESE CRACKER CRUMBS   ½ cup
PARMESAN CHEESE   1 tablespoon grated
PAPRIKA   1 teaspoon
MARGARINE

Mix carrots, onions, pimentos, parsley, tarragon, and mushrooms together. Sprinkle trout with salt inside and out. Arrange trout in greased 9 x 13-inch pan. Fill with stuffing mixture and spread leftover on top. Pour melted margarine over trout, then wine. Cover with a buttered brown paper bag, cut open; bake at 425° for 10 minutes. Remove and discard bag. In a paper bag mix crumbs, cheese, and paprika; sprinkle over fish. Dot with bits of margarine. Broil for a few minutes until browned. Serves 4 to 6.

QUICK CRAB QUICHE

BACON SLICES   3
ONION   ½ cup chopped
FLOUR   1 tablespoon
SWISS CHEESE   1 cup shredded
PASTRY   for 1-crust 9-inch pie
CRAB MEAT or MINCED CLAMS   ½ cup
CARROTS   1 cup cooked and sliced
GREEN PEPPER   2 tablespoons finely minced
CARAWAY SEED   1 tablespoon (optional)
WHOLE EGGS   3, beaten
EVAPORATED MILK or HALF-AND-HALF   1 cup
MAYONNAISE   ½ cup
SALT   ½ teaspoon
NUTMEG   ¼ teaspoon

Fry bacon crisp. Drain on paper towels and crumble. Saute onion in 1 tablespoon of bacon fat. Mix flour with cheese and spread on unbaked pie crust. Layer with crab, then carrots, green pepper, and caraway seed. Sprinkle with bacon and onion. Mix rest of ingredients together. Pour over mixture in pie pan. Bake at 450° for 10 minutes. Reduce heat to 325° for another 15 minutes until set. Do not overbake. Serves 6 to 8.

SHERRIED SHRIMP CURRY

ONION   1 cup sliced
MARGARINE   3 tablespoons
SALT   1 teaspoon
CURRY POWDER   1 tablespoon
VINEGAR   1 teaspoon
SUGAR   1 teaspoon
WORCESTERSHIRE SAUCE   1 teaspoon
YOGURT   1 cup
CONDENSED CREAM OF TOMATO SOUP   2 10½-ounce cans
SHERRY   ⅓ cup
CARROTS   1 cup cooked and diced
SHRIMP   2 pounds, shelled and cleaned
RICE   cooked
APPLE   1, peeled and diced

Saute onion in margarine. Add rest of ingredients except shrimp, rice, and apple. Cook for 10 minutes. Add shrimp and cook until shrimp are tender. Serve on hot rice; sprinkle with apple. Serves 8.

BRAZILIAN VATAPA

SHRIMP   1 pound, shelled and cleaned
FISH FILLETS   1 pound
TOMATOES   1 cup peeled and sliced
ONION   ½ cup minced
GARLIC CLOVE   1, minced
OREGANO   ½ teaspoon
VEGETABLE OIL   ¼ cup
CARROTS   ½ cup shredded and chopped
CREAM OF RICE CEREAL   ¼ to ½ cup
COCONUT MILK*   2 cups
HOT PEPPER SAUCE   dash
RICE   cooked
CASHEWS   ½ cup coarsely chopped

Cook shrimp and fish separately in as little water as possible. Flake the fish. Make a sauce by simmering tomatoes, onions, garlic, oregano, and oil. Press through a sieve. Add the fish, shrimp, carrots, and more water if too thick. Then add cereal, coconut milk, and pepper sauce. Flavor improves as it simmers. Serve on hot rice; sprinkle with cashews. Serves 8.

Note: This is an adaptation of a traditional Brazilian dish.

*Add 2 cups hot milk to 1 cup flaked coconut. Let stand until cool; squeeze milk through cheesecloth.

GOURMET OYSTER-CARROT BAKE

OYSTERS   1 10-ounce jar with liquid
CONDENSED CREAM OF MUSHROOM SOUP   1 10½-ounce
                                                                        can

CARROTS   ½ cup shredded and chopped
GREEN ONIONS WITH TOPS   3, chopped
LEMON JUICE   2 tablespoons
DRY WHITE WINE   3 tablespoons
SALT and PEPPER   to taste
BREAD CRUMBS   ½ cup, herbed and buttered*
PARSLEY SPRIG   1, chopped
RICE   cooked

Chop oysters coarsely. Bring to a boil in their liquid and simmer for
5 minutes. Add next 6 ingredients; simmer for another 5 minutes.
Spoon into greased 1-quart casserole; top with crumbs and parsley.
Bake at 350° for 10 minutes until bubbling hot. Spoon over hot rice.
Serves 4.

* Saute crumbs in margarine, stirring in ¼ teaspoon thyme,
marjoram, or oregano.

Oyster-Carrot Soup: Dilute with 2 cups of clam nectar to make a
delicious soup for 6. Sprinkle each bowl with crumbs and parsley.

FRED SALING'S CLAM BAKE SANDWICH

THICK WHOLE-WHEAT or RYE BREAD SLICES   4, toasted
BUTTER
CLAMS   1 7-ounce can, drained and minced
MADEIRA or SHERRY   4 tablespoons
CHICKEN BROTH CREAM SAUCE
PARMESAN CHEESE   ¼ cup grated

Butter the toast and cut to fit into 4 greased individual casseroles. Spread each piece of toast with clams; sprinkle with wine. Pour cream sauce over and sprinkle with cheese. Bake at 400° for 7 to 10 minutes until piping hot. Serves 4.

CHICKEN BROTH CREAM SAUCE

MARGARINE   3 tablespoons
FLOUR   3 tablespoons
CHICKEN BROTH   2 cups
BAY LEAF   ½
CAYENNE   dash
CARROTS   ¼ cup blender-chopped
LEMON JUICE   1 tablespoon
YOGURT   ¼ cup
GREEN ONION WITH TOPS   1, chopped

Make white sauce of margarine, flour, and chicken broth. Add bay leaf, cayenne, and carrots. Simmer 5 to 10 minutes until quite thick. Remove bay leaf; add remaining ingredients.

CURRIED SALMON LOAF

SALMON   1 1-pound can, drained and flaked
BREAD CRUMBS or COOKED RICE   1 cup
PIMENTOS   1 2-ounce jar, chopped
CARROTS   1 cup blender-chopped
YOGURT   ½ cup
SHARP CHEDDAR CHEESE   1 cup
CELERY   ½ cup chopped
GARLIC CLOVE   1, minced
WHOLE EGGS   2
HOT CURRIED WHITE SAUCE   1 cup
PICKLE RELISH or SWEET PICKLES   ½ cup chopped
BREAD CRUMBS   herbed and buttered*
HOT CURRIED WHITE SAUCE   topping

Mix all ingredients together except crumbs. Press into greased 9 x 5-inch loaf pan. Sprinkle with crumbs. Bake at 375° for about 1 hour. Serve with more white sauce.

* Saute dry bread crumbs in margarine, stirring in ¼ teaspoon thyme or rosemary.

Note: To make hot curried white sauce, add curry powder to white sauce.

SAVORY SALMON PATTIES

SALMON   1 7-ounce can, drained and flaked
CARROTS   1 cup shredded and chopped
ONION   ¼ cup minced
GREEN PEPPER   3 tablespoons chopped
RIPE OLIVES   3 tablespoons chopped
CONDENSED CREAM OF MUSHROOM SOUP   ½ 10½-ounce
                                                    can

WORCESTERSHIRE SAUCE   1 teaspoon
DRY BREAD or CRACKER CRUMBS   2 cups
THYME   ½ teaspoon
WHOLE EGGS   2
PREPARED MUSTARD   1 teaspoon
MARGARINE or BACON FAT
CHEESE WHITE SAUCE

Mix all ingredients together, except margarine and white sauce, adding more crumbs if too moist. Form into 6 patties and fry in margarine. Serve with cheese white sauce. Serves 6.

Note: *To make cheese white sauce, add grated cheese to white sauce.*

DILLY TUNA BAKE

CONDENSED CREAM OF MUSHROOM SOUP   1 10½-ounce
                                                        can

DRY WHITE WINE   ½ cup
FRENCH-FRIED POTATOES
TUNA   1 7-ounce can, drained and flaked
CARROTS   1 cup shredded
WHOLE EGGS   2, hard-cooked and sliced
ONION   ¼ cup minced
DILL WEED   1 teaspoon
SALT   ½ teaspoon
PEPPER   ⅛ teaspoon coarsely ground
PAPRIKA   ¼ teaspoon
CRACKER CRUMBS   1 cup, buttered and cheesed*

Mix soup with wine; simmer until hot. In a greased 1½-quart casserole, layer potatoes, tuna, carrots, and eggs, sprinkling each layer with onion and seasonings. Pour hot soup mixture over top. Sprinkle with crumbs. Bake at 350° for 20 to 25 minutes. Serves 6.

* Saute crumbs in 3 tablespoons margarine and add 2 teaspoons grated Parmesan cheese.

88

Pickles
Relishes
Marmalades

CARROT CHUTNEY

ORANGES   2
LEMON   1
CARROTS   3 cups cooked and coarsely diced
PICKLING SPICES   1 tablespoon
ONION   ½ cup chopped
RAISINS   1 cup
TART APPLES   1 cup chopped
BROWN SUGAR   2 cups firmly packed
GINGER ROOT   1 teaspoon grated
WATER   ½ cup
VINEGAR   ¼ cup
GARLIC CLOVE   1, minced
PECANS or WALNUTS   ¼ cup chopped
SALT   1 teaspoon
CAYENNE   dash
MUSTARD SEED   1 teaspoon

Peel oranges and lemon thinly with vegetable peeler, discarding any membrane. Chop peel finely. Cut membrane away from fruit and discard; slice fruit thinly, removing seeds. Combine all ingredients and simmer for 20 to 30 minutes, stirring often. Seal in 3 hot sterilized pint jars.

CARROT POTPOURRI RELISH

CARROTS   2 cups coarsely blender-chopped
CUCUMBERS   1 cup chopped
ONION   ¾ cup chopped
CABBAGE   1 cup finely shredded
SWEET RED PEPPER   ¾ cup chopped
GREEN TOMATOES   1 cup coarsely ground
CELERY   ½ cup chopped
ZUCCHINI   1 cup chopped
PICKLING SALT   1 cup
BROWN SUGAR   1 cup firmly packed
SUGAR   1 cup
CIDER VINEGAR   2 cups
TURMERIC   1 tablespoon
CAYENNE   ⅛ teaspoon
ALLSPICE   1 teaspoon
GINGER   ½ teaspoon
CLOVES   ½ teaspoon
MUSTARD SEED   3 tablespoons
CELERY SEED   2 tablespoons
GARLIC CLOVE   1, minced

Combine all vegetables with pickling salt in crock, enamel or stainless steel pan and let stand overnight. Then drain and rinse. Bring sugar, vinegar, and seasonings to a boil. Add vegetables and bring to a boil again. Simmer for 15 minutes. Pack into 5 hot sterilized pint jars and seal. Process 15 minutes in boiling water bath.

MIXED GARDEN PICKLE RELISH

CARROTS   5 cups cooked and diced
CUCUMBERS   4 cups peeled and chopped
SMALL CAULIFLOWER   1, chopped
GREEN PEPPERS   2, chopped
ONIONS   1 cup chopped
FLOUR   2 tablespoons
SUGAR   1 cup
SALT   4 teaspoons
CELERY SEED   1 tablespoon
GARLIC CLOVE   1, minced
DRY MUSTARD   1½ teaspoons
TURMERIC   1 teaspoon
PAPRIKA   1 teaspoon
CIDER VINEGAR   1½ cups
WATER   1 cup

Combine vegetables. Mix dry ingredients together; add to vinegar and water. Bring to a boil. Add vegetables; simmer until slightly thick. Seal in 8 hot pint jars. Process 15 minutes in boiling water bath.

OVERNIGHT CARROT RELISH

CARROTS   1 cup blender-chopped
CABBAGE   1 cup finely shredded
ONION   ¼ cup chopped
TOMATOES   1 cup peeled and coarsely chopped
SALT   1 teaspoon
SUGAR   1 tablespoon
WINE VINEGAR   ¼ cup
WATER   ¼ cup, ice cold
OLIVE OIL   3 tablespoons

Stir all ingredients together except oil. Chill overnight in tightly covered bowl. Then add oil. Serve with meat or hamburgers. Makes 4 cups.

CARROT CHILI SAUCE

CARROTS   4 cups shredded and chopped
TOMATOES   1 cup peeled and chopped
CELERY   ¾ cup chopped
GREEN PEPPER   1, chopped
MEDIUM ONION   1, chopped
SUGAR   1½ cups
SALT   2 teaspoons
CLOVES   ¼ teaspoon
PAPRIKA   ½ teaspoon
TURMERIC   ¼ teaspoon
ALLSPICE   ½ teaspoon
MUSTARD SEED   1 tablespoon
VINEGAR   2 cups

Simmer carrots and tomatoes together in a little water until carrots are tender. Add rest of ingredients and boil until thick, about 1 hour, stirring to prevent burning. Pour into 4 hot sterilized pint jars; seal.

SEAFOOD COCKTAIL SAUCE

MAYONNAISE   ½ *cup*
YOGURT   ½ *cup*
CARROTS   ¼ *cup shredded and chopped*
DRY HORSERADISH   *1 tablespoon*
TABASCO SAUCE   *2 drops*
CATSUP   ½ *cup*
WORCESTERSHIRE SAUCE   *1 tablespoon*
TARRAGON WINE VINEGAR   *2 tablespoons*
MADEIRA or SHERRY   *2 tablespoons*
CELERY   ¼ *cup chopped*
GREEN ONIONS WITH TOPS   *2, chopped*
WHOLE EGG   *1, hard-cooked and chopped*

Mix all ingredients together and chill. Pour over seafood Louis salad or seafood cocktail. Makes 2½ cups.

CARROT SAUERKRAUT

CARROTS   *coarsely shredded*
SALT
CABBAGE   *shredded (optional)*

Place carrots in a stone crock, sprinkling salt on each layer and pressing down until a brine appears. Brine must cover carrots. If it evaporates during fermentation, add more salt. Cabbage can be added also; always sprinkle with salt. A weight on the top will keep vegetables under the brine. Let ferment for several weeks at least. Can be used cooked or raw. Take out what you need, wash it in cold water, and cook with pork or ham until tender.

PICKLED CARROTS CALIENTE

CARROTS   6, cooked and cut in strips
OLIVE OIL   3 tablespoons
GARLIC CLOVE   1, minced
HOT CHILI PEPPER   1, quartered
SALT   ½ teaspoon
WINE VINEGAR   2 cups

Put carrots in a quart canning jar. Combine all ingredients except vinegar and pour over carrots. Cover with vinegar and let stand for several days. Keeps well. Makes 1 quart.

HAWAIIAN JAM

CARROTS   2 cups shredded and chopped
CRUSHED PINEAPPLE   1 cup drained
FRESH APRICOTS   1 cup chopped
LEMON JUICE   3 tablespoons
SUGAR   3 cups
GINGER ROOT   1 teaspoon finely grated
ALMONDS or WALNUTS   ½ cup chopped

Mix carrots, fruit, and lemon juice together in heavy 4-quart kettle. Heat to boiling, stirring occasionally so that it does not burn. Add sugar gradually; add ginger root. Cook, stirring often, for 30 to 40 minutes until of jam consistency. Remove and add nuts. Pour into 6 sterilized 6-ounce glasses; seal.

LEMONY WINE MARMALADE

SUGAR   2½ cups
CARROTS   2 cups shredded and chopped
LEMONS   2, juice and grated rind
GINGER ROOT   2 teaspoons shredded
DRY RED WINE   ¼ cup

Mix sugar with carrots. Add lemon juice and rind and ginger root to carrots. Cook slowly about ½ hour until carrots are cooked and mixture is thick. Add wine the last 10 minutes. Pour into 4 hot 6-ounce sterilized jars; seal.

NEW ZEALAND ORANGE-CARROT MARMALADE

CARROTS   2 cups coarsely ground
LARGE ORANGES   3
LEMONS   2
SUGAR   about 2 pounds
WALNUTS   1 cup coarsely chopped (optional)

Cook carrots in a little water for 15 to 20 minutes until tender. Juice the oranges and lemons; peel them as thinly as possible with vegetable peeler, discarding any membrane; grind peel. Add juice and peel to carrots; measure. Add ⅔ cup sugar to each cup of carrot mixture. Simmer in preserving kettle, stirring constantly, until it thickens. Add nuts at last minute. Pour into 4 hot 6-ounce sterilized jars; seal.

Soups
Sandwiches
Salads

CARROT BORSCHT

BEEF STEW MEAT   1 pound, cut in cubes
ONION   ½ cup chopped
MARGARINE   3 tablespoons
TOMATO JUICE   2 cups
BAY LEAF   1
PEPPERCORNS   4
CARROTS   3 cups shredded
CONDENSED CREAM OF TOMATO SOUP   1 10½-ounce can
SALT   1 teaspoon
YOGURT   ½ cup
DILL WEED   1 tablespoon chopped

Brown meat and onion in margarine in pressure cooker. Add tomato juice, bay leaf, and peppercorns. Cook under pressure 15 minutes; remove bay leaf and peppercorns. Place meat in blender with some of broth; whirl (or chop finely). Return it to pressure cooker, add carrots and cook until tender. Add soup and salt; reheat to boiling point. Serve with spoonful of yogurt and a sprinkle of dill. Serves 4 to 6.

SOUP SUPREME

GARLIC CLOVE   1
GREEN ONIONS WITH TOPS   ¼ cup minced
MARGARINE   1 tablespoon
CHUNKY PEANUT BUTTER   ½ cup
CARROTS   1 cup blender-chopped
CONDENSED CREAM OF CELERY SOUP   1 10½-ounce can
CHICKEN BROTH or BOUILLON   1½ cups
SALT   1 teaspoon
WORCESTERSHIRE SAUCE   ¼ teaspoon
PARSLEY SPRIGS   2, chopped
CROUTONS
MARGARINE

Saute garlic and onion in margarine; add peanut butter to blend. Add next 6 ingredients; simmer 10 to 15 minutes to blend flavors. If desired, thicken with flour mixed with water. Serve with croutons fried in margarine. Serves 4.

SOUP A LA GARBANZO

GARBANZOS   1 1-pound can
CONDENSED CONSOMME or BEEF BOUILLON   1 10½-
ounce can
ONION   ½ cup chopped
GREEN PEPPER   ½, chopped
CARROTS   ½ cup chopped
WORCESTERSHIRE SAUCE   2 teaspoons
CELERY STALK WITH LEAVES   1, chopped
TOMATOES   1 20-ounce can
SALT   ½ teaspoon
PEPPER   to taste
THYME   ½ teaspoon
YOGURT   1 cup
SHARP CHEDDAR CHEESE   grated
BEEF SAUSAGE SLICES or TINY MEAT BALLS

Mix first 11 ingredients together; cook for 20 minutes until celery
and carrots are tender. Add yogurt and heat. To make a 1-dish meal,
sprinkle with cheese and garnish with meat. Serves 8.

HEARTY BEEF SOUP POT

GROUND BEEF   1 pound
MEDIUM ONION   1, chopped
MARGARINE   3 tablespoons
CONSOMME or BEEF BOUILLON   4 cups
TOMATO JUICE or STEWED TOMATOES   3 cups (whirl
                                    tomatoes in blender)

THYME   ½ teaspoon
CELERY   ¼ cup chopped
CARROTS   3 cups shredded
SALT and PEPPER   to taste
WORCESTERSHIRE SAUCE   1 teaspoon
PARMESAN CHEESE   ¼ cup grated

Saute beef and onion in margarine until browned. Pour off excess
fat. Add rest of ingredients except cheese. Simmer 35 minutes.
Sprinkle with cheese. Serves 8 to 10.

DIETER'S CARROT BOUILLON

CHICKEN BOUILLON CUBE   1
WATER or TOMATO JUICE   1 cup, boiling
ONION   1 teaspoon minced
CELERY   1 tablespoon minced
CARROTS   1 tablespoon finely grated
WORCESTERSHIRE SAUCE   ½ teaspoon

Dissolve bouillon cube in water. Add remaining ingredients. Heat to
boiling. Serves 1.

BOMBAY CHICKEN CURRY SANDWICH

CHICKEN MEAT   2 cups cooked and finely diced
CARROTS   ¾ cup blender-chopped
ONION   ¼ cup minced
GREEN PEPPER   1 tablespoon minced
CURRY POWDER   ¼ teaspoon
SALT   ½ teaspoon
MAYONNAISE   ½ cup

Mix well.

PUGET SOUND SALMON SANDWICH

SALMON   2 cups cooked and flaked
WHOLE EGG   1, hard-cooked and chopped
CARROTS   ½ cup blender-chopped
GREEN ONIONS WITH TOPS   ¼ cup chopped
CAPERS   1 tablespoon
DAIRY SOUR CREAM   ½ cup

Mix well.

SWISS-TOMATO SANDWICH

SWISS CHEESE   1 cup shredded
TOMATO   ½ cup peeled and chopped
CARROTS   ½ cup blender-chopped
GREEN ONIONS WITH TOPS   ¼ cup minced
CELERY STALK   1, finely chopped
MAYONNAISE   ½ cup

Mix well.

CREAM CHEESE DELI SANDWICH

CARROTS   ½ cup shredded and chopped
WALNUTS or PEANUTS   ½ cup chopped
CREAM CHEESE   1 4-ounce package, creamed with
YOGURT   1 tablespoon
MARGARINE   2 tablespoons, soft
MAYONNAISE   ¼ cup

Mix well.

GOLDEN CHEDDAR SANDWICH

SHARP CHEDDAR CHEESE   1 cup shredded
CARROTS   ½ cup shredded and chopped
MARGARINE   ¼ cup, soft
PREPARED MUSTARD   1 teaspoon
WORCESTERSHIRE SAUCE   1 teaspoon
PAPRIKA   ⅛ teaspoon
MAYONNAISE   ½ cup

Mix well.

CARROTOCADO SANDWICH

AVOCADO   1, peeled and mashed
LEMON JUICE   1 tablespoon
GREEN ONIONS WITH TOPS   2, chopped
CARROTS   ¼ cup shredded and chopped
WALNUTS   ¼ cup chopped
FRENCH DRESSING   ¼ cup

Mix well.

CLAM ISLANDER SANDWICH

CLAMS   ½ cup minced
BACON BITS   2 tablespoons
CARROTS   ¼ cup shredded and chopped
MAYONNAISE   to moisten

Mix well.

PEANUT CRUNCH SANDWICH

CRUNCHY PEANUT BUTTER   ½ cup
MARGARINE   4 tablespoons
MAYONNAISE   4 tablespoons
CARROTS   ½ cup shredded and chopped
BACON BITS   garnish

Mix well.

EGG-BACON SANDWICH

WHOLE EGGS   2, hard-cooked and chopped
CARROTS   ¼ cup shredded and chopped
BACON BITS   2 tablespoons
MARGARINE   2 tablespoons
MAYONNAISE   to moisten

Mix well.

BLACK FOREST MIXED SALAD

FRENCH DRESSING ¼ *cup*
MAYONNAISE ¼ *cup*
CARROTS 2 *cups cooked and sliced*
MEDIUM BERMUDA ONION ⅓, *sliced in thin rings*
PARSLEY SPRIGS 2, *chopped*
CELERY STALKS 2, *finely chopped*
CABBAGE ¼ *cup finely chopped*
DILL PICKLE 1 *tablespoon chopped*
WHOLE EGG 1, *hard-cooked and diced*
LETTUCE

Mix French dressing and mayonnaise together; add rest of ingredients except lettuce and mix well. Refrigerate for an hour so flavors blend. Serve on lettuce. Serves 4.

CRISP AND CRUNCHY VEGETABLE SALAD

CAULIFLOWER 1 *cup finely chopped*
ONION 2 *teaspoons minced*
CELERY 1 *cup finely chopped*
TART APPLE 1, *chopped*
CARROTS 1 *cup blender-chopped*
WALNUTS 1 *cup finely chopped*
MAYONNAISE 1 *cup*
LEMON JUICE 1 *tablespoon*
WALNUTS 4 *to 6, halved*

Mix all ingredients together, reserving a few walnuts for garnish. Serves 4 to 6.

GREEN AND GOLD SALAD

PEAS   1 cup cooked
MARINATED CARROTS*   1 cup
CELERY   ½ cup chopped
SHARP CHEDDAR CHEESE.   ½ cup cubed
WHOLE EGGS   2, hard-cooked and chopped
SALT   ¼ teaspoon
DRESSING FROM MARINATED CARROTS

Mix all ingredients together and let flavors blend in refrigerator for
several hours. Stir occasionally. Serves 4.

*See recipe in appetizer section.

GUACAMOLE MOLD

UNFLAVORED GELATIN   1 envelope
WATER   1 cup, cold
LEMON JUICE   3 tablespoons
ONION   1 teaspoon finely chopped
WHOLE EGGS   2, hard-cooked and chopped
CARROTS   1 cup shredded and chopped
RIPE OLIVES   ¼ cup minced
CAPERS   1 tablespoon chopped
GARLIC SALT   ¼ teaspoon
AVOCADOS   2, peeled and mashed
MAYONNAISE   ½ cup

Soften gelatin in water and then set cup in hot water until gelatin is
dissolved. Let chill; mix rest of ingredients together. When gelatin is
cold, blend in mixture. Spoon into 1½-quart mold that has been
rinsed in cold water. Chill until firm. Serves 6.

Note: A 7-ounce can of tuna may be added for a supper main dish.

HIGH-PROTEIN BEAN SALAD

MAYONNAISE   ½ cup
PREPARED MUSTARD   1 teaspoon
CHILI SAUCE   ½ cup
KIDNEY BEANS   1 16-ounce can, drained
CARROTS   1 cup shredded
CELERY   ½ cup sliced
RED CABBAGE   1 cup finely sliced
WHOLE EGGS   2, hard-cooked and chopped
BLACK OLIVES   ½ cup, halved
BERMUDA ONION   ⅓ cup thinly sliced
GREEN PEPPER   ⅓ cup finely chopped
SHARP CHEDDAR CHEESE   ½ cup cubed
DILL PICKLE   ½ cup coarsely chopped
WALNUTS   ½ cup chopped
SALT   1 teaspoon
PEPPER   ¼ teaspoon coarsely ground

Mix mayonnaise with mustard and chili sauce; combine with rest of ingredients. Chill for several hours, stirring occasionally. Serves 6 to 8.

AVOCADO-EGG SALAD

AVOCADO   1, peeled and diced
CARROTS   ¼ cup blender-chopped
WHOLE EGGS   4, hard-cooked and chopped
SHARP CHEDDAR CHEESE   ¼ cup chopped
LEMON JUICE   1 tablespoon
MAYONNAISE   ½ cup
SALT and PEPPER   to taste
BASIL   ½ teaspoon crumbled
RIPE OLIVES   4 whole, pitted

Mix all ingredients together. Garnish with olives. Serves 4.

COOL CRUMBED SALAD

DRY WHOLE-WHEAT BREAD CRUMBS   1 cup
MARGARINE   4 tablespoons, melted
WALNUTS or PEANUTS   ½ cup chopped
CARROTS   2 cups shredded
VEGETABLE OIL   4 tablespoons
TARRAGON WINE VINEGAR   2 tablespoons
SALT   1 teaspoon
PAPRIKA   ⅛ teaspoon
CHERVIL   ½ teaspoon

Saute crumbs in margarine until crumbs are well coated. Remove from heat. Add nuts and carrots. Mix remaining ingredients together; drizzle over salad. Chill. Serves 4.

CRUNCHY SALAD

CARROTS   1 cup blender-chopped
ONION   2 tablespoons, minced
WALNUTS   ½ cup coarsely chopped
CELERY STALK   1, chopped
WHOLE EGGS   2, hard-cooked and chopped
PAPRIKA   ¼ teaspoon
MAYONNAISE   to moisten

Mix all ingredients together. Chill before serving. Serves 2.

RICE TOSS SALADE

CARROTS   1 cup cooked and sliced
FRENCH DRESSING   ¾ cup
RICE   2 cups cooked and chilled
CELERY   1 cup chopped
WHOLE EGGS   3, hard-cooked and chopped
GREEN ONIONS WITH TOPS   3, chopped
PEAS   ½ cup cooked
DILL WEED   ½ teaspoon
SALT   to taste
PEPPER   ⅛ teaspoon coarsely ground

Marinate carrots in French dressing for several hours. Then mix all ingredients together and chill for several hours. Serves 4.

Note: *A can of tuna with its oil is a good addition.*

CHILLED PORK-VEGETABLE DELIGHT

PORK ROAST   1 cup cooked and diced
CARROTS   1 cup cooked and diced
POTATOES   ½ cup cooked and diced
GREEN BEANS   ½ cup cooked
WHOLE EGGS   2, hard-cooked and coarsely chopped
CHERRY TOMATOES   1 cup halved
CELERY   ½ cup finely chopped
ONION   2 tablespoons minced
MEDIUM DILL PICKLE   1, coarsely diced
MAYONNAISE   ¼ cup
FRENCH DRESSING   ¼ cup
SAGE   ⅛ teaspoon
POPPY SEED   1 tablespoon
PEPPER   ¼ teaspoon coarsely ground
SALT   to taste
PAPRIKA   ⅛ teaspoon

Mix all ingredients together and chill for several hours so flavors blend. Serves 4.

TANGY SALMON TOSS

MAYONNAISE   ½ cup
FRENCH DRESSING   ¼ cup
VINEGAR   2 tablespoons
SALMON   1 1-pound can, drained and flaked
CABBAGE   1 cup finely shredded
CARROTS   1 cup blender-chopped
ONION   ¼ cup minced
SWISS CHEESE   ½ cup cubed
CAPERS   2 tablespoons
SALT   1 teaspoon
PEPPER   ½ teaspoon coarsely ground
WHOLE EGG   1, hard-cooked and sliced

Mix mayonnaise, French dressing, and vinegar together. Combine rest of ingredients except egg. Toss salad with dressing. Garnish with egg. Serves 6.

MOCK SALMON SALAD

TOMATOES   4
TUNA   1 7-ounce can, drained and flaked
CARROTS   3, shredded and finely chopped
ONION   3 tablespoons grated
WALNUTS   ¼ cup finely chopped
MAYONNAISE   ⅓ cup

Slice off top half inch of tomatoes. Scoop out pulp; chop pulp and mix with rest of ingredients. Stuff tomatoes with mixture.

Or serve on lettuce, as canape spread, to fill lunch meat roll-ups, or in deviled egg filling. Serves 4.

TUNA-CARROT RAVIGOTE

TUNA   1 7-ounce can, drained and flaked
CARROTS   ½ cup shredded and chopped
WHOLE EGG   1, hard-cooked and finely chopped
PREPARED MUSTARD   2 teaspoons
CAYENNE   ⅛ teaspoon
CAPERS   1 tablespoon
PARSLEY SPRIG   1, chopped
TARRAGON WINE VINEGAR   ¼ cup
OLIVE OIL   3 tablespoons
DRY WHITE WINE   3 tablespoons
PEPPER   ⅛ teaspoon coarsely ground
SALT   to taste

Mix all ingredients together. Serve on lettuce as salad, or stuff avocado or tomato with mixture. Serves 4.

Vegetables
Side Dishes
Stuffings

CARROTS MARSALA

ONION   ½ cup minced
GARLIC CLOVE   1, minced
VEGETABLE OIL   2 tablespoons
CHICKEN BROTH   1 cup
SALT   1 teaspoon
CARROTS   1 cup blender-chopped
CELERY STALK   1, chopped
EGG YOLKS   2
NUTMEG   ¼ teaspoon
MARSALA, MADEIRA, or SHERRY   ¼ cup
PARSLEY SPRIGS   2, chopped

Saute onion and garlic in oil until golden. Add broth, salt, and vegetables. Simmer, covered, for 20 to 25 minutes, until tender-crisp. Remove vegetables from pan and keep warm. Mix egg yolks, nutmeg, and wine. Stir some of hot mixture in pan into yolks. Then stir yolk mixture into mixture in pan. Cook until thickens. Add vegetables for a few minutes to heat. Sprinkle with parsley. Serves 4.

DIJON-WINE CARROTS

GREEN ONIONS WITH TOPS   *2, chopped*
MARGARINE   *2 tablespoons*
DIJON MUSTARD   *2 tablespoons*
DRY WHITE WINE   *¼ cup*
CARROTS   *2 cups cooked and sliced*

Saute onions in margarine. Add mustard mixed with wine. Add carrots and simmer until hot. Serves 4.

WINE-CAPER CARROTS

DRY WHITE WINE   *1 tablespoon*
MARGARINE   *2 tablespoons*
WATER   *1 tablespoon*
GARLIC CLOVE   *½, minced*
DRY MUSTARD   *¼ teaspoon*
CAPERS   *1 tablespoon chopped*
CARROTS   *2 cups shredded*

Mix all ingredients together. Cook, covered, until carrots are barely tender. Serves 4.

SHERRIED CRUMBED CARROTS

CARROTS   8, cooked and quartered
WHOLE EGG   1
WATER   1 tablespoon
DRY WHOLE-WHEAT BREAD CRUMBS   1 cup
VEGETABLE OIL
CONDENSED CREAM OF MUSHROOM SOUP   1 10½-ounce
                                                                            can
SHERRY   2 tablespoons
PARSLEY SPRIG   1, chopped
YOGURT   ½ cup
DILL WEED   2 tablespoons

Cook carrots until almost tender. Beat egg and water together. Dip carrots in egg mixture, and then in crumbs. Fry in deep hot fat until light brown. Then put in a shallow greased casserole. Heat soup with sherry; pour over carrots. Bake at 350° for 10 minutes. Sprinkle with chopped parsley. Or serve with yogurt and dill. Serves 8.

Note: Cooked carrots can also be fried in deep hot fat without dipping in crumbs first. Insert a sprig of parsley in end to make look like fresh foliage.

CONSOMME CARROTS IN WINE

ONION   ¼ cup minced
GARLIC CLOVE   ½, minced
MARGARINE   2 tablespoons
FLOUR   2 tablespoons
CONSOMME or BEEF BOUILLON   ¼ cup
DRY WHITE WINE   3 tablespoons
CARROTS   2 cups cooked and julienned
CAPERS   1 tablespoon drained

Saute onion and garlic in margarine. Stir in flour, consomme, and wine. Heat; add carrots and capers. Cook until thickened and hot. Serves 4.

WINE-LEMON GLAZED CARROTS

CARROTS   2 cups cooked and sliced
MARGARINE   2 tablespoons
SWEET RED WINE   1½ cups
LEMON JUICE   2 tablespoons

Saute carrots in margarine. Add wine and lemon juice. Simmer until well glazed. Serves 4.

ONION-CARROTS AU VIN

GREEN ONIONS WITH TOPS   6, chopped
MARGARINE   ¼ cup
DRY WHITE WINE   ¾ cup
CARROTS   2 cups cooked and sliced (or julienned)
BROWN GRAVY   1 cup
LEMON JUICE   2 tablespoons

Saute onions in margarine. Add wine and carrots; simmer 10 minutes. Add gravy and lemon juice; simmer another 5 minutes. Serves 4.

VIN-CAPER CARROTS

CARROTS   2 cups cooked and sliced
DRY WHITE WINE   ¼ cup
DAIRY SOUR CREAM   ¼ cup
CAPERS   1 tablespoon drained

Simmer carrots in wine until hot. Add sour cream and capers. Heat through. Serves 4.

CRANBERRY-WINE CARROTS

DRY RED WINE   ¼ cup
CRANBERRIES   1 cup
CRUSHED PINEAPPLE   ½ cup drained
CELERY   ¼ cup minced
MARGARINE   3 tablespoons
SALT   ¼ teaspoon
HONEY   ⅔ cup
WATER   ¼ cup
CARROTS   2 cups cooked and sliced
WALNUTS   ½ cup chopped

Cook all ingredients together except carrots and nuts until heated through. Add carrots and simmer, stirring, for 10 minutes. Add nuts. Serves 6.

SAUCY SHERRY CARROTS

MARGARINE   2 tablespoons
HONEY or BROWN SUGAR   1 tablespoon
SALT   ½ teaspoon
LEMON RIND   ½ teaspoon grated
SHERRY   ¼ cup
LEMON JUICE   1 tablespoon
CARROTS   3 cups shredded
WALNUTS   ¼ cup chopped

Mix all ingredients together except carrots and nuts. Simmer carrots in sauce for 10 minutes. Add nuts. Serves 6.

CHILI CARROTS

GARLIC CLOVE   ½, minced
ONION   ¼ cup minced
CELERY   3 tablespoons finely minced
MARGARINE   2 tablespoons
CARROTS   2 cups cooked and sliced
CHILI SAUCE   ¼ cup

Saute garlic, onion, and celery in margarine. Add carrots and chili sauce. Simmer for 10 minutes. Serves 4.

SOUTHERN HAM FRITTERS

CARROTS   2 cups cooked and mashed
HAM   ⅓ cup finely chopped
ONION   1 tablespoon grated
DRY BREAD CRUMBS   ½ cup
WHOLE EGG   1, beaten
EVAPORATED MILK   ¼ cup
PARSLEY   1 tablespoon minced
DRY BREAD CRUMBS
VEGETABLE OIL or MARGARINE

Mix all ingredients together except crumbs and oil. Shape into fritters. Dip in crumbs and chill. Fry in deep hot fat at 375° for 3 minutes. Drain on paper towels. Makes 6 to 8.

HAM-STUFFED CARROT BOATS

LARGE CARROTS   *6, whole*
SALT and PEPPER
HAM   *⅓ cup ground*
MAYONNAISE   *¼ cup*
ONION   *2 tablespoons*
PICKLE RELISH   *1 tablespoon*
CRUMBS   *½ cup, buttered*
MARGARINE   *¼ cup, melted*
PAPRIKA   *¼ teaspoon*

Cook carrots until nearly tender in pressure cooker for 5 minutes. Cut a thin slice lengthwise from each carrot. Make a shell ¼-inch thick by carefully cutting around edge with thin knife, such as a grapefruit knife, and scooping out pulp with spoon. Reserve pulp. Sprinkle shell with salt and pepper. Chop carrot pulp. Add ham, mayonnaise, onion, and relish; mix well. Stuff shells. Sprinkle with crumbs; then drizzle with margarine and sprinkle with paprika. Bake in a shallow greased pan with ¼-inch water in bottom at 350° for 20 to 30 minutes. Serves 6.

CELERY CARROTS

BACON SLICES   4
CARROTS   2 cups cooked and sliced
CELERY   ¾ cup chopped
GREEN PEPPER   ½, chopped
ONION   ½ cup chopped
FLOUR   3 tablespoons
SALT   1 teaspoon
BEEF BOUILLON   1 cup
TOMATO SAUCE   1 8-ounce can (optional)

Fry bacon crisp. Remove and drain on paper towels; crumble. In bacon fat saute vegetables until soft; mix in bacon. Place vegetable mixture in greased 1½-quart casserole. Sprinkle with flour mixed with salt. Add bouillon and tomato sauce. Bake at 350° for 30 to 40 minutes. Serves 6 to 8.

CHEESE CARROTS

MARGARINE   3 tablespoons, melted
CARROTS   2 cups cooked and sliced
PARMESAN CHEESE   3 tablespoons grated
PAPRIKA   ¼ teaspoon

Pour margarine over carrots, sprinkle with cheese and paprika. Brown briefly under broiler. Serves 4.

CABBAGE-CARROT DUET

CABBAGE   2 cups finely shredded
CARROTS   1 cup shredded
CHICKEN BROTH   1 cup
PREPARED MUSTARD   1 teaspoon
SALT   ½ teaspoon
SUGAR   2 tablespoons
VINEGAR   3 tablespoons
PAPRIKA   ¼ teaspoon
MARGARINE   ⅓ cup, melted
EVAPORATED MILK   3 tablespoons

Simmer vegetables in chicken broth until tender. Mix rest of ingredients together and add. Reheat. Serves 6.

CURRIED CARROT TIMBALES

ONION 1 tablespoon minced
MARGARINE or BACON FAT 3 tablespoons
FLOUR 2 tablespoons
CELERY SALT ¼ teaspoon
CURRY POWDER ½ teaspoon
EVAPORATED MILK 1 cup
WHOLE EGGS 3, slightly beaten
CARROTS 2 cups cooked and mashed
GREEN PEPPER 1 tablespoon minced
PAPRIKA ⅛ teaspoon
SALT ¼ teaspoon

Saute onion in margarine. Stir in flour, celery salt, and curry powder. Add milk gradually, stirring until thick. Stir a little of sauce into eggs. Then stir egg mixture into sauce. Add remaining ingredients; mix well. Spoon into 6 greased custard cups. Set them in a pan of hot water and bake at 350° for 30 minutes until firm. Serves 6.

Note: For a lighter timbale, separate eggs and fold beaten yolks into sauce first. Then fold in stiffly beaten whites at the last minute.

CURRIED MUSHROOM CARROTS

MARGARINE   *3 tablespoons, melted*
CURRY POWDER   ½ to 1 teaspoon
LEMON JUICE   1 teaspoon
CARROTS   3 cups shredded
CHICKEN BROTH   ½ cup
PARSLEY   2 tablespoons chopped
MUSHROOMS   ½ cup

Mix margarine, curry powder, and lemon juice. Saute carrots in mixture to brown lightly. Add broth and cook, covered, for 25 minutes. Add parsley and mushrooms and cook 5 minutes more. Serves 6.

ONION-CURRY CARROTS

CARROTS   2 cups shredded
GREEN ONIONS WITH TOPS   1 cup chopped
SALT   ½ teaspoon
CURRY POWDER   ½ teaspoon
CHICKEN BROTH   ½ cup
MARGARINE   3 tablespoons
EVAPORATED MILK   ½ cup, heated

Mix all ingredients together except milk in greased 1-quart casserole. Cover and bake at 350° for 30 minutes. Stir in milk. Serves 4.

SOY SAUCY CARROTS

CARROTS   2 cups shredded
BACON FAT   3 tablespoons
SOY SAUCE   1 tablespoon
SUGAR   1 tablespoon
WATER   1 tablespoon

Saute carrots in bacon fat. Add soy sauce, sugar, and water. Simmer until tender. Serves 4.

COCONUT-CURRIED CARROTS

ONION   1, chopped
BACON FAT   2 tablespoons
FLOUR   2 tablespoons
CURRY POWDER   1 to 2 teaspoons
CHICKEN BROTH   1 cup
TART APPLE   1, peeled and chopped
COCONUT MILK*   2 cups
CARROTS   4 cups cooked and sliced
SALT   to taste
WHOLE EGG   1, hard-cooked and sliced

Saute onion in bacon fat. Add flour and curry powder. Gradually add chicken broth and apple. Stir in coconut milk; simmer 10 minutes. Add carrots; salt to taste and heat through. Garnish with egg. Serves 4 to 6.

*Add 2 cups boiling water to 1 cup flaked coconut. Let stand until cool; squeeze milk through cheesecloth.

CHICKEN-SEASONED CASSEROLE

SMALL ONION   1, grated
MARGARINE or BACON FAT   3 tablespoons
CARROTS   3 cups shredded or thinly sliced
PARSLEY   ¼ cup minced
FLOUR   2 tablespoons
CHICKEN BROTH or BOUILLON   1 cup, well seasoned
DRY BREAD CRUMBS   ¾ cup
WORCESTERSHIRE SAUCE   1 teaspoon
PAPRIKA   ¼ teaspoon
SALT and PEPPER   to taste
PARMESAN CHEESE   grated

Saute onion in margarine until soft. Add carrots and parsley; cook 5 minutes, stirring. Stir in flour; add chicken broth gradually. Stir in rest of ingredients except cheese. Spoon into greased, covered 2-quart casserole. Bake at 400° for 40 to 50 minutes, until liquid is almost absorbed. Sprinkle with cheese before serving. Serves 4 to 6.

HONEY-CHEESE CARROTS

CARROTS   2 cups cooked and halved
HONEY   ½ cup
SALT   1 teaspoon
PARMESAN CHEESE   ¼ cup grated

Dip carrots in honey, sprinkle with salt, and cover with cheese. Bake at 400° for 10 minutes. Serves 4.

HOLIDAY CRANBERRY-ORANGE CARROTS

CARROTS   2 cups cooked and sliced
MARGARINE   3 tablespoons
BROWN SUGAR   3 tablespoons
CRANBERRY-ORANGE RELISH   ½ cup, uncooked

Heat all ingredients together and simmer, stirring, for 10 minutes. Serves 4.

CHEESY CARROTS A LA CREME

MARGARINE   2 tablespoons
SUGAR   1 teaspoon
SALT   ½ teaspoon
CHICKEN BROTH   1 cup
CARROTS   2 cups sliced
ONION   ¼ cup minced
WHOLE EGGS   2, well beaten
CREAM or EVAPORATED MILK   ½ cup
SHARP CHEDDAR CHEESE   2 tablespoons grated
PARSLEY   2 teaspoons chopped

Mix first 4 ingredients together. Simmer carrots and onion in broth mixture until tender. Mix remaining ingredients together. Add to carrot mixture; heat well. Thicken with a little flour if desired. Serves 4.

HERB-CRUMBED BAKE

WHOLE EGG   1
WATER   1 tablespoon
MEDIUM CARROTS   4, cooked and quartered
CORN FLAKES or DRY BREAD CRUMBS   ¾ cup
MARJORAM   ½ teaspoon
PARMESAN CHEESE   2 tablespoons grated
MARGARINE   4 tablespoons, soft
PARSLEY   4 tablespoons minced

Beat egg with water. Dip warm carrots in egg mixture and then in crumbs mixed with marjoram and cheese. Place in shallow greased casserole and bake at 450° for 10 to 15 minutes. To serve, brush with margarine and sprinkle with parsley. Serves 4 to 6.

HOT CARROT CAESAR

WHOLE-WHEAT BREAD CUBES   1 cup
VEGETABLE OIL   3 tablespoons
VINEGAR   1 tablespoon
VEGETABLE OIL   1 tablespoon
GARLIC CLOVE   1, minced
ONION   2 tablespoons minced
CARROTS   1 cup cooked and cubed
CELERY STALK   1, finely chopped
SALT   ½ teaspoon
PARMESAN CHEESE   ¼ cup grated

In skillet saute bread cubes in oil until crisp and golden; remove cubes. Put rest of ingredients except cheese in skillet, and stir until hot. Add cubes and sprinkle with cheese. Serves 4.

TARRAGON TREAT

CARROTS   2 cups cooked and sliced
MARGARINE   3 tablespoons
SUGAR   2 teaspoons
SALT   2 teaspoons
PEPPER   ⅛ teaspoon
CHICKEN BOUILLON CUBE   1
WATER   ¼ cup, hot
LETTUCE LEAVES   4, wet
TARRAGON   1 teaspoon
PARSLEY   1 tablespoon chopped

Saute carrots in margarine, sugar, salt, and pepper. Add the bouillon cube dissolved in water. Cover with lettuce leaves and cook, covered, over low heat for 20 minutes. Remove lettuce; add tarragon and parsley. Cook for 5 minutes more. Serves 4.

ZUCCHINI-CARROTS ITALIANO

GARLIC CLOVE   1, minced
OLIVE OIL   3 tablespoons
CARROTS   1 cup shredded
ONION   ½ cup chopped
ZUCCHINI   1 cup shredded
THYME   ½ teaspoon
OREGANO   ½ teaspoon
BEEF BOUILLON   3 tablespoons
PARMESAN CHEESE   3 tablespoons grated
PARSLEY   1 tablespoon chopped

Saute garlic in oil. Add rest of ingredients except cheese and parsley; simmer until tender. Top with cheese and parsley. Serves 4.

CARROT-ORANGE COMBO

MARGARINE   2 tablespoons
BROWN SUGAR   2 tablespoons
ORANGE   1, peeled and cut in segments, membrane removed
CARROTS   2 cups cooked and julienned

Melt margarine; add sugar and orange. Then add carrots and cook slowly to glaze. Serves 4.

APPLE-CARROT PIQUANT

LEMON JUICE   2 tablespoons
LEMON RIND   1 teaspoon grated
BROWN SUGAR   3 tablespoons
SALT   ½ teaspoon
CINNAMON   ¼ teaspoon
NUTMEG   ¼ teaspoon
MARGARINE   3 tablespoons, melted
TART APPLES   1½ cups peeled and sliced
CARROTS   1½ cups cooked and sliced
SHARP CHEDDAR CHEESE   ½ cup shredded

Mix first 7 ingredients together. In a greased 1-quart casserole, alternate slices of apple and carrots, sprinkling each layer with a little of the lemon mixture. Cover and bake at 350° for 25 minutes. Uncover, sprinkle with cheese and bake for another 5 minutes. Serves 4.

Savory Apple-Carrot Bake: *Saute 1 thinly sliced large onion in ¼ cup margarine and layer it with other ingredients. Add ¼ teaspoon sage and omit cinnamon and nutmeg.*

CARROTS A LA ROMA

MARGARINE   4 tablespoons, melted
TOMATO PASTE   2 tablespoons
SALT   ½ teaspoon
MARJORAM   ½ teaspoon
CARROTS   3 cups cooked and sliced
SHARP CHEDDAR CHEESE   ½ cup

Blend all ingredients together except carrots and cheese. Mix carrots in sauce. Bake in greased, covered 1-quart casserole at 350° for 15 minutes. Sprinkle with cheese and bake uncovered for 5 minutes more. Serves 6.

FIERY MUSTARD CARROTS

MAYONNAISE   ¼ cup
PREPARED MUSTARD   1 teaspoon
PREPARED HORSERADISH   1 teaspoon
VINEGAR   1 teaspoon
SUGAR   ½ teaspoon
SALT   to taste
CARROTS   2 cups cooked and shredded

Mix all ingredients together. Simmer until hot. Serves 4.

ROSEMARY-BACON CARROTS

MARGARINE   3 tablespoons
ONION   3 tablespoons chopped
ROSEMARY   ¼ teaspoon crumbled
LEMON JUICE   2 tablespoons
BACON   ¼ cup fried crisp and crumbled
CARROTS   2 cups cooked and mashed (or shredded and par-
boiled)

Mix all ingredients together and heat in double boiler.

DILLY DELIGHT

ONION   ½ cup chopped
MARGARINE   3 tablespoons
CARROTS   2 cups cooked and sliced
BROWN SUGAR   1 tablespoon
WATER   4 tablespoons
DAIRY SOUR CREAM   1 cup
DILL WEED or PARSLEY   2 tablespoons

*Saute onion in margarine. Add carrots, sugar, and water; simmer
15 minutes. Add sour cream mixed with dill. Serves 4.*

NUTTY CARROTS

CARROTS   2 cups cooked and julienned
WALNUTS   ½ cup chopped
ONION SALT   ¼ teaspoon
CELERY SALT   ¼ teaspoon
GARLIC SALT   ¼ teaspoon

Saute all ingredients together until hot. Serves 4.

ALLSPICE CARROTS

MARGARINE   2 tablespoons
HONEY   2 tablespoons
LEMON JUICE   2 tablespoons
LEMON RIND   ½ teaspoon grated
SALT   ½ teaspoon
ALLSPICE   ¼ teaspoon
CARROTS   3 cups cooked and sliced

In saucepan, mix all ingredients together except carrots. Simmer sauce for a few minutes. Add carrots and heat through.

Note: Substitute 1 teaspoon crushed caraway seed for allspice.

LEMON CREAMED CARROTS

CARROTS   2 cups cooked
MARGARINE   3 tablespoons
MAYONNAISE   1 cup
DAIRY SOUR CREAM   ½ cup
LEMON JUICE   1 teaspoon
CHIVES   1 teaspoon
DILL WEED or CELERY SEED   ½ teaspoon

Braise carrots in margarine. Mix remaining ingredients together and heat. Add carrots and heat through. Serves 4.

SWEET-SOUR CREAMED CARROTS

CARROTS   2 cups cooked and mashed
HONEY   4 tablespoons
LEMON JUICE   3 tablespoons
FLOUR   1 tablespoon
SALT   ½ teaspoon
NUTMEG   ½ teaspoon
DAIRY SOUR CREAM   ½ cup

Mix all ingredients together except sour cream. Heat in double boiler. Stir in sour cream and heat through. Serves 4 to 6.

DILLED CARROTS

CARROTS   2 cups cooked julienned or baby whole
MARGARINE   3 tablespoons
ONION SALT   1 teaspoon
DILL WEED   3 tablespoons chopped

Coat carrots with melted margarine; sprinkle with onion salt. Roll in dill weed. Serve hot. Serves 4.

GINGER-LEMON CARROTS

LEMON JUICE   1 teaspoon
LEMON RIND   ½ teaspoon grated
SALT   ¾ teaspoon
HONEY   1 tablespoon
GINGER   ½ teaspoon
MARGARINE   2 tablespoons, melted
CARROTS   3 cups cooked and sliced

Mix all ingredients together except carrots in a small saucepan. Heat and pour over carrots. Bake in a greased, covered 1-quart casserole at 350° for 30 minutes. Serves 6.

Lemon Carrots: To 3 tablespoons carrot cooking water, add ⅓ cup honey, 2 teaspoons lemon juice, and ½ teaspoon salt. Cook 20 to 30 minutes. Blend 1 tablespoon flour into 2 tablespoons margarine and add to sauce to thicken.

CARROTS ELEGANTE

CARROTS   2 cups cooked and mashed, hot
MARGARINE   4 tablespoons
EVAPORATED MILK   ¼ cup, heated
SALT   ½ teaspoon
NUTMEG   ¼ teaspoon
ALMONDS   1 tablespoon slivered and toasted

Whip all ingredients together except almonds until light. Heat until piping hot in double boiler. Sprinkle with almonds when serving. Serves 6.

ONION-DILL CARROTS

CARROTS   3 cups cooked and mashed
ONION   1 cup cooked and sliced
CREAM   4 tablespoons
MARGARINE   2 tablespoons
SUGAR   1 teaspoon
SALT   ½ teaspoon
DILL WEED   1 teaspoon

Mash all ingredients together and beat smooth. Reheat in double boiler. Serves 6.

PINEAPPLE-CARROT FLUFF

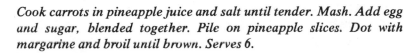

CARROTS   3 cups sliced
PINEAPPLE JUICE   ¼ cup
SALT   ¼ teaspoon
WHOLE EGG   1, slightly beaten
BROWN SUGAR   2 tablespoons
PINEAPPLE SLICES   6, drained
MARGARINE   2 tablespoons

Cook carrots in pineapple juice and salt until tender. Mash. Add egg and sugar, blended together. Pile on pineapple slices. Dot with margarine and broil until brown. Serves 6.

WHIPPED CARROT-POTATO FLUFF

CARROTS   1 cup cooked and mashed
POTATOES   1 cup cooked and mashed
CREAM or EVAPORATED MILK   ½ cup
EGG YOLK   1
MARGARINE   2 tablespoons
PREPARED MUSTARD   1 teaspoon
GREEN ONION WITH TOPS   1 tablespoon minced
PARSLEY   1 tablespoon chopped
PARMESAN CHEESE   2 tablespoons grated
SALT   to taste

Mix hot vegetables with other ingredients. Heat in double boiler until hot. Serves 4.

Note: *Can be used as "crust" on top of a casserole, browned under broiler for a few minutes.*

PIMENTO-GREEN BEAN CARROTS

BACON SLICES   4
ONION   ¼ cup chopped
GREEN PEPPER   2 tablespoons chopped
PIMENTO   1, minced
LEMON JUICE   1 teaspoon
CARROTS   1 cup cooked and sliced
GREEN BEANS   1 cup cooked
MARJORAM   ⅛ teaspoon
ROSEMARY   ⅛ teaspoon

Fry bacon. Remove and drain on paper towels; crumble. Saute onion and green pepper in bacon fat. Add rest of ingredients; cook for 5 minutes. Sprinkle with bacon. Serves 4.

ROSEMARY-BEAN CARROTS

ONION   ¼ cup minced
CARROTS   1 cup sliced
STRING BEANS   1 cup cut in 2-inch lengths
CHICKEN BROTH   ½ cup
MARGARINE   2 tablespoons
SALT   1 teaspoon
ROSEMARY   ¼ teaspoon
CORNSTARCH   2 teaspoons
WATER   2 tablespoons, cold

Cook vegetables with chicken broth, margarine, salt, and rosemary, until tender. Blend cornstarch and water; stir into vegetable liquid. Cook until sauce thickens. Serves 4.

GREEN BEAN-MUSTARD CARROTS

GREEN ONIONS WITH TOPS   ⅓ cup thinly sliced
MARGARINE   2 tablespoons
PREPARED MUSTARD   1 teaspoon
WORCESTERSHIRE SAUCE   1 teaspoon
SALT   ¼ teaspoon
GREEN BEANS   1 cup cooked
CARROTS   1 cup cooked and sliced
BREAD CRUMBS   herbed and buttered*

Saute onions in margarine. Cream together mustard, Worcester-shire sauce, and salt; mix with onions. Stir in drained, hot vegetables; let simmer for 5 minutes. Sprinkle with crumbs just before serving. Serves 4.

* Add ¼ teaspoon thyme, marjoram, or oregano to crumbs while sauteing them.

LEMON-MINT CARROTS

CARROTS   *2 cups cooked and sliced*
CORNSTARCH   *1 teaspoon*
SUGAR   *1 tablespoon*
WATER   *⅓ cup*
LEMON RIND   *½ teaspoon grated*
MARGARINE   *2 tablespoons*
LEMON JUICE   *1 teaspoon*
MINT LEAVES   *1 tablespoon chopped*

Simmer carrots until hot in sauce made of remaining ingredients. Serves 4.

CITRUS CARROTS

CARROTS   *2 cups cooked and diagonally sliced*
GRAPEFRUIT, TANGERINE, or ORANGE   *1 cup sliced*
MARGARINE   *4 tablespoons*
HONEY   *¼ cup*
ORANGE RIND   *1 teaspoon grated*
CLOVES   *¼ teaspoon*

In a greased 1-quart casserole, alternate carrot and fruit slices, drizzling each layer with mixture of margarine, honey, orange rind, and cloves. Bake at 350° for 30 minutes. Serves 6.

ONION-LEMON CARROTS

MEDIUM ONION   *1, chopped*
MARGARINE   *3 tablespoons*
BREAD CRUMBS or FLOUR   *4 tablespoons*
BEEF or CHICKEN BOUILLON   *1 cup*
PAPRIKA   *¼ teaspoon*
SALT   *½ teaspoon*
PARSLEY   *1 tablespoon chopped*
LEMON JUICE   *1 tablespoon*
CARROTS   *2 cups cooked and sliced*

Saute onion in margarine; stir in crumbs. Gradually add remaining ingredients. Simmer until thick. Serves 4.

CARROTS TROPICALE

CARROTS   *3 cups julienned*
CRUSHED PINEAPPLE or TIDBITS   *1 cup drained, reserve juice*
ORANGE RIND   *1 tablespoon grated*
BROWN SUGAR   *½ cup firmly packed*
CINNAMON   *¼ teaspoon*
LEMON JUICE   *1 tablespoon*
MARGARINE   *¼ cup*
CORNSTARCH   *2 tablespoons*
WALNUTS   *¼ cup chopped*

Cook carrots in pineapple juice until tender. Add remaining ingredients, except for cornstarch and nuts. Cook slowly, stirring, for 10 minutes. If desired, thicken with cornstarch mixed with a little water. Then add nuts. Serves 8.

TANGY CARROTS

YOGURT   1 cup
PREPARED HORSERADISH   1 to 2 tablespoons
CHIVES   2 tablespoons chopped
SALT   ½ teaspoon
CARROTS   3 cups cooked and sliced

Blend first 4 ingredients and pour over hot carrots. Serves 6.

CRUMBED CARROTS

CARROTS   2 cups cooked and julienned
MARGARINE   3 tablespoons
DRY BREAD CRUMBS   ½ cup
PARMESAN CHEESE   2 tablespoons grated
THYME or MARJORAM or favorite herb   ¼ teaspoon
BACON SLICE   1, fried crisp and crumbled

Saute carrots in margarine. Mix crumbs, cheese, and thyme together. Add to carrots and heat, shaking pan to mix. Top with bacon. Serves 4.

SWEET-SOUR GLAZED CARROTS

FLOUR   2 *tablespoons*
MARGARINE   ¼ *cup*
BROWN SUGAR or HONEY   2 *tablespoons*
ALLSPICE   ½ *teaspoon*
SALT   ½ *teaspoon*
RED WINE or LEMON JUICE   ¼ *cup*
LEMON RIND   2 *teaspoons grated*
TINY CARROTS   2 *cups cooked whole or julienned*
CARROT WATER   1 *cup*

Blend flour into melted margarine in saucepan. Add remaining ingredients; cook until thickened. Bake in greased 1-quart casserole at 350° for 10 minutes.

MUSTARD GLAZED CARROTS

TINY CARROTS   2 *cups cooked whole or julienned*
MARGARINE   2 *tablespoons*
BROWN SUGAR   2 *tablespoons*
PREPARED MUSTARD   1 *teaspoon*

Simmer all ingredients together for about 10 minutes, until carrots are glazed.

GREEN PEPPER GLAZED CARROTS

GREEN PEPPER   1, diced
MARGARINE   4 tablespoons
TINY CARROTS   2 cups cooked whole or julienned
SUGAR   1 tablespoon
NUTMEG   ⅛ teaspoon
SALT   ½ teaspoon

*Saute pepper in margarine for 5 minutes. Mix in other ingredients;
cook for another 5 or 6 minutes.*

GINGER-PINEAPPLE GLAZED CARROTS

MARGARINE   3 tablespoons
PINEAPPLE JUICE   1 cup
CHICKEN BOUILLON CUBE   1
LEMON RIND   ½ teaspoon grated
GINGER ROOT   1 teaspoon shredded
BROWN SUGAR   4 tablespoons
CARROTS   2 cups shredded or julienned

*Combine all ingredients. Cook carrots until sauce is all absorbed.
Then cook for several minutes more, shaking pan, until carrots are
glazed.*

SHERRIED GLAZED CARROTS

CARROTS   2 cups shredded
BROWN SUGAR   1 tablespoon
MARGARINE   2 tablespoons
SALT   ½ teaspoon
SHERRY   ¼ cup
PECANS   ¼ cup chopped

Simmer all ingredients together except pecans for 10 minutes in covered saucepan. Sprinkle with pecans.

HONEY-MINT GLAZED CARROTS

HONEY   2 tablespoons
MARGARINE   3 tablespoons
ORANGE RIND   1 teaspoon grated
TINY CARROTS   2 cups cooked whole or julienned
MINT LEAVES   2 tablespoons chopped (optional)

Simmer all ingredients together except mint for about 10 minutes, until carrots are glazed. Add mint during last minute of cooking, or sprinkle over at serving time.

APRICOT JAM GLAZED CARROTS

CARROTS   1 cup sliced
SMALL PICKLING ONIONS   1 cup
CELERY   ½ cup minced
SALT   1 teaspoon
CHICKEN BROTH   ½ cup
MARGARINE   2 tablespoons
APRICOT JAM   ½ cup

Cook vegetables in salt and chicken broth. Then glaze in margarine and jam.

OATMEAL TURKEY STUFFING

QUICK-COOKING OATS   5 cups
ONION   1 cup chopped
CELERY   1 cup chopped
CARROTS   1 cup shredded
PARSLEY   3 tablespoons minced
POULTRY SEASONING   1 to 2 teaspoons
SALT   1 teaspoon
MARGARINE   ⅓ cup, melted
CHICKEN BROTH   2 tablespoons

Toast oats under broiler on baking sheet for 2 minutes. Mix with remaining ingredients. Add enough chicken broth so that stuffing holds together when squeezed. Makes 8 cups; enough for 8-pound turkey.

SAVORY CELERY STUFFING

ONION   ⅓ cup chopped
MARGARINE   1 tablespoon
CELERY   1 cup finely chopped
CARROTS   1 cup shredded
SALT   1 teaspoon
PARSLEY   ¼ cup chopped
POULTRY SEASONING   ½ teaspoon
SOFT BREAD CRUMBS   2 cups
BACON SLICES   2, fried crisp and crumbled
CHICKEN BROTH or BOUILLON   1 tablespoon

Saute onion in margarine. Add rest of ingredients. Add enough chicken bouillon so that stuffing holds together when squeezed. Cook for about 5 minutes. Makes 4½ cups; enough for 4 Cornish hens or 2 roasting chickens.

SAUSAGE-CORNBREAD STUFFING

PORK SAUSAGE   *½ pound*
ONION   *1½ cups chopped*
GREEN PEPPER   *½, chopped*
CELERY   *1 cup chopped*
CARROTS   *1 cup shredded*
CORNBREAD   *2 8-inch square pans full, crumbled*
POULTRY SEASONING   *2 teaspoons*
SALT   *2 teaspoons*
WALNUTS   *1 cup coarsely chopped*
CHICKEN BROTH or BOUILLON   *1 cup*

Fry sausage until done; remove from pan. In sausage fat, saute onion, green pepper, and celery until golden. Add carrots, cornbread, seasonings, and nuts. Stir well. Moisten with chicken broth, using just enough so that stuffing holds together when squeezed. Makes 12 cups; enough for a 14- to 16-pound turkey.

Index

POULTRY

SEAFOOD

MAIN DISHES, MEATLESS

Ann Saling, a free-lance writer and staff writer for PACIFIC SEARCH magazine, was a Navy wife for 21 years. She has traveled widely and lived in Hawaii, Chile, and Brazil, where she experimented with exotic foods and pursued her favorite hobby of cooking.

Darci Covington, a Northwest free-lance illustrator, is a University of Washington student and illustrator for the University newspaper.